The Open University

Business School

Block 6: Contemporary directions in strategy

This publication forms part of the Open University module B301 *Making sense of strategy*. The complete list of texts which make up this module can be found at the back (where applicable). Details of this and other Open University modules can be obtained from the Student Registration and Enquiry Service, The Open University, PO Box 197, Milton Keynes MK7 6BJ, United Kingdom (tel. +44 (0)300 303 5303; email general-enquiries@open.ac.uk).

Alternatively, you may visit the Open University website at www.open.ac.uk where you can learn more about the wide range of modules and packs offered at all levels by The Open University.

To purchase a selection of Open University materials visit www.ouw.co.uk, or contact Open University Worldwide, Walton Hall, Milton Keynes MK7 6AA, United Kingdom for a catalogue (tel. +44 (0)1908 274066; fax +44 (0)1908 858787; email ouw-customer-services@open.ac.uk).

The Open University, Walton Hall, Milton Keynes MK7 6AA

First published 2010. Second edition 2014.

Edited and designed by The Open University.

Typeset by The Open University.

Printed and bound in the UK by Page Bros, Norwich.

ISBN 978 1 4730 2375 8

3.1

Contents

Introduction to Block 6

This final block of the module looks to the future in two ways. In Unit 1, we explore scenario planning, a way in which strategists can try to make sense of the possible futures into which their organisations may be moving. In doing this we are building on work you have already done in Block 2 on environmental analysis – but with the difference that we are looking at how strategists can respond to the challenge of forecasting events, not just over the relatively near future, but over much longer periods.

We then move from looking at the future in general to a much more specific, and academic, focus on some of the directions in which strategy itself is travelling as a field of thought and research. Unit 2 aims to give you an overview of developments in thinking, which may become more widely accepted as orthodoxy as we move through the twenty-first century. We have chosen to focus on two emerging perspectives in particular. The first, 'strategy as practice', has already featured in our discussions in Blocks 1 and 5. As you will recall, this approach to making sense of strategy begins with studying what strategists actually do. In Unit 2, we look in particular at how strategy activities often centre on telling stories of one sort or another. An understanding of the role of narrative in strategy work can help support better ways to encourage and facilitate the development of strategy in an organisation.

Strategy as practice is a way of understanding strategy that takes its inspiration from the social sciences. Complexity theory, the second emerging perspective on which we focus in Unit 2, takes its inspiration from the natural sciences. It sees organisations and their activities as complex systems, which organically adapt themselves to changing conditions. This way of seeing strategy is particularly appropriate for the complex and often unstable environments in which contemporary strategists have to form and carry out their plans.

The final section of Unit 2 explores the relationship between strategy and society. First we turn to the relatively recent field of critical management studies. Throughout the module, we have been asking you to be critical in your approach to understanding concepts and models – seeing them in context with their respective limitations instead of accepting them as universally true. By doing so, we hope, you will have a clearer appreciation of their genuine value and be able to use them more effectively. Critical management studies (CMS) applies a critical perspective not so much to individual ideas but to the whole way that management has developed as a discipline, suggesting it is time to re-evaluate its impact on human and environmental welfare. As you may gather, it is a controversial area, but one which has a direct bearing on the ethical and practical application of strategic thinking. We then move on to another perspective on business and society: corporate social responsibility (CSR). Instead of arguing for radical power shift advocated by CMS, CSR argues that with the right strategy businesses can behave as good citizens within the current political and economic system. Michael Porter's most recent work has been in this field, where he has managed to preserve his broadly 'classical' stance on strategy by pointing out what he sees as the mutual interests of business and society.

Learning outcomes

This block contributes towards the following learning outcomes:

Knowledge and understanding

- of the nature of strategy and the issues it raises for organisations (module learning outcome 1)

- of how organisations respond to the challenges of environmental change (module learning outcome 2)

- of a range of policy and environmental concepts and issues which demonstrate the impact of the macroenvironment on organisations (module learning outcome 5).

Cognitive skills

- critical thinking, analysis and synthesis; including identifying and questioning assumptions, weighing evidence appropriately, identifying and challenging false logic or reasoning, and generalising in a way which recognises the limits of knowledge in strategy (module learning outcome 8)

- evaluation and comparison of competing perspectives from a variety of sources, including some informed by current issues or research developments (module learning outcome 9)

- the ability to argue relevantly and justify a point of view (module learning outcome 10).

Key skills

- communication of complex information, arguments and ideas in ways appropriate to a business context and audience (module learning outcome 11)

- problem solving and decision making using appropriate quantitative and qualitative skills, including data analysis, interpretation and extrapolation (module learning outcome 12)

- effective performance in a team environment in a virtual context (module learning outcome 13)

- selecting and using information and communication technologies for business purposes (module learning outcome 14).

Practical and professional skills

- engagement, as appropriate, with practical and professional business strategy skills and ethical issues (module learning outcome 16).

Unit 1: Strategy and the future

Aims

Success can take many forms. For a commercial firm, it is likely to involve growth and profitability or perhaps just long-term survival. For a non-profit organisation, such as a school or hospital, a satisfactory financial result is still necessary, but is accompanied by targets such as numbers of pupils on roll, exam results, or numbers of patients treated and treatment success rates.

Whatever their definition of success, all organisations share the need to sustain a successful performance into the longer term. In a sense, the future is what all strategies have in common. What really distinguishes leading organisations is their ability to hold on to success, to achieve 'sustainable competitive advantage'. This means that all strategists have to address the issue of the future, and need to design strategy and implementation to be as future-proof as possible.

The future for any organisation involves a measure of risk and uncertainty. Risk is something that we can quantify – on the understanding that we can assess the probability of foreseen circumstances. Uncertainty, on the other hand, is less easily quantified. It concerns outcomes that may be unforeseen, or those which are foreseen but against which a degree of estimated risk cannot be set. By its very nature, it eludes our attempts to put an order of magnitude on it. In Unit 2, while acknowledging the importance of judgement, we take the discussion further by putting forward several ways in which strategists can attempt to get a clearer sense of the futures they face – foreseeable and otherwise.

After studying this unit, you should be able to:

- comment on the role of forecasting in how organisations respond to the challenges of environmental change
- use and explain methods by which organisations interpret the future impact of macroenvironmental factors on their strategies
- explain the use and value of scenario planning as a strategic tool.

1.1: Forecasting

One of the differences between businesses in the West and their Asian counterparts is a sense of timescale. American and European investors have traditionally been keen to make relatively speedy returns on their investments, whereas Japanese firms tend to take a longer view (Jain and Tucker, 1995). There is an accompanying sense of short-termism about how businesses are talked about and evaluated in English-language news media.

Consider the way in which the news media that you personally use cover business. Understandably news editors favour recent events and dramatic incidents over long-term trends, so their pages and programmes tend to focus exclusively on the short term. Even specialist financial journalism aimed at professional investors tends to concentrate on quarterly results and forecasts – sending share prices soaring or plunging as the market communicates its confidence (or lack of it) in the relevant companies.

A short-term perspective is by no means the sole preserve of commercial organisations. Many not-for-profit (NFP) organisations – whether statutory or voluntary – depend on funding arrangements that are renewed annually and support for specific projects, which have limited lives. Furthermore, policy developments, which can have a profound effect on the long-term futures of public sector and voluntary organisations, are prone to being announced suddenly by politicians who are themselves locked in short-term survival games. This means that, even though the outcomes, intentions and effects of all but a very few commercial and voluntary organisations are long term by nature, there is a temptation for management thinking, supported by systems and operations, to focus on this year or the next as a planning horizon. Strategy focuses organisations on the long term – rising above the day-to-day concerns of operational issues to see beyond them. Forecasting is a logical consequence of a focus on the long term, as strategists attempt to estimate future conditions in order to guide appropriate present and future activity.

Before moving on to a discussion of forecasting methods, it is worth pausing to clarify a potential confusion in terminology. In many organisations, the terms 'forecasting' and 'budgeting' are used interchangeably. Alternatively, they may be used to describe different aspects of essentially the same thing – as in a sales forecast for the coming year (income) supported by a sales budget for the same period (expenditure). However, there is an important – and useful – difference between the two terms, properly speaking. As we have stated in the previous paragraph, a forecast is an attempt to estimate what will happen in the future. It will be based on assumptions, but it is meant to be unbiased – a neutral view of what is likely to happen.

Budgeting, on the other hand, expresses what the organisation specifically intends to happen through its planned actions. Obviously, this is a less 'neutral' view of the future. What the organisation considers achievable – which may not be the same as what the forecast indicates is possible – will constrain the budget. The principle of 'under-promise and over-deliver' (Templar, 2005) often holds true in budgeting – but forecasting should be innocent of any such political intention.

To sum up, the forecast is the basis for planning – the budget is the organisation's response, its commitment to action. The forecast needs to be as accurate and unbiased as possible – a common thread in all the methods we will review in the following material is the way each one tries to avoid bias. The budget needs to be practical and achievable, which means that it will take into account the difficulties of implementation and the fact that, once a target is named, accountability is created. The sequence should be one of neutral, unbiased forecast, feeding into calculated, deliberate budget, resulting in action.

1.2: Quantitative forecasting methods

Traditionally, forecasting methods have fallen into two broad types – quantitative and qualitative (terms which will be familiar to you if you have studied marketing research).

Quantitative methods deal in numbers, as inputs and outputs. This gives them at least the appearance of rigour and objectivity. It is worth remembering that whenever you are making a case for investment or justifying a business decision, being able to present credible-looking figures is something that can be very persuasive to an audience. But the advantages of a quantitative approach are not confined to making a convincing case. Figures require you to quantify your plans, and such quantification encourages coherence and consistency. A 'reality check' can save a lot of wasted time and effort further along the planning process by eliminating some ideas as less feasible than others at an early stage.

Quantitative forecasting depends on the availability of systematically collected historical data – known as time-series data. Time-series data consist of clearly-defined items of data measured over regular periods of time. So, for example, four-weekly figures for car production is a time series – it's quite clear what the data items are (production figures in a particular industry where it is possible to define what is being measured – here cars rather than other vehicles), and it is also quite clear that the measurement takes place at regular intervals 13 times a year.

Computer packages have made sophisticated data analysis widely available to managers concerned with quantitative forecasting. This is to be welcomed as long as it does not lead to an exaggerated or naive faith in the forecasts that emerge. In fact, one of the potential advantages of quantitative forecasting is the way it acknowledges and puts an order of magnitude on its potential inaccuracy. Such forecasts come qualified with an estimate of their reliability within a stated range, known as a prediction interval. An example might be a forecast with a declared 90 per cent chance of containing the true value of what is being predicted. Even equipped with the most sophisticated quantitative techniques, therefore, strategists have to use their own interpretative skills and judgement.

Makridakis et al. (1998) divide quantitative forecasts into two kinds: time-series and explanatory. The difference between them is quite straightforward. With a time-series forecast, you simply try to predict future behaviour from what has happened in the past. There is no attempt to understand the cause of the behaviour – merely to recognise a pattern from the data and project it into the future to support your forecast. Whatever is producing the pattern is regarded as a 'black box' whose inner workings are not investigated. Only its results are of interest (as in Box 1.1). It might be that the reasons for what is happening appear too complicated to allow cost-effective measurement and calculation, or it might simply be that all you want to do is predict and attempt to control events rather than understand them. You are simply looking for patterns, which can be projected into the future.

Box 1.1: Spotting a trend?

During the eighteenth, nineteenth, and first part of the twentieth centuries [...] there were several people concerned with the magnitude of sunspots. There was little known at that time as to the reasons for the sunspots or the sources of energy of the sun. This lack of knowledge, however, did not hinder many investigators who collected and analysed the frequency of sunspots. Schuster (1906) found that there was a regular pattern in the magnitude of sunspots, and he and several others were able to predict their continuation through time-series analysis.

(Source: Makridakis et al., 1998, p. 11)

Explanatory forecasts, on the other hand, are concerned with how and why change happens – hence the term 'explanatory'. They rest on theories of how changes in some factors contributing to a situation are linked to changes in other factors present in the same situation. Because the emphasis is on how things change (or vary), these factors are called 'variables'. Depending on what you are trying to explain (and thus predict) variables are divided into 'independent' and 'dependent'. Changes in the dependent variable depend on changes in the value of the independent variable(s). In spite of the slightly misleading terminology of 'dependence' (as in 'it depends'), this is not to say that such relationships are necessarily directly causal. They may be, but all we can say for certain is that they demonstrate a correlation – in other words, a change in one will be accompanied by a change in the other.

For example, it may be that a person's willingness to give money to charity increases with their age, or where they live. This makes explanatory sense. As we get older we may become more prosperous and our values may change so that we are more inclined to be generous. Also, similar people tend to live in similar neighbourhoods (hence the power of geodemographic targeting where marketers segment their customers by postcode area). However, age and geography do not in themselves cause someone to give to charity. One 60-year-old may be much more generous than another even though they live in the same street. Just moving to a different area will not affect how much money you give away. Nevertheless, in planning fundraising strategy, charity managers take into account the correlations between factors such as age and geography that past data demonstrate, and predict their targets accordingly. Box 1.2 provides an example of the difference between a cause and a correlation from my personal experience.

Box 1.2: Give a tree a bad name

I was recently in South Africa working with a group of managers and academic colleagues at a residential school. The management centre we were using was set in beautiful grounds, and we spent our breaks outside enjoying the wonderful weather. One of my colleagues drew my attention to a very handsome tree, about 15 metres tall with feathery dark-green foliage and a light-green bark. 'That's a fever tree', he said, 'There used to be a lot more of them at one time'. He explained that the tree was suspected of causing fever (hence the name) because of the number of people who caught malaria in areas where it grew in large numbers. Only after substantial numbers of the tree were cut down by early settlers did it become apparent that what was causing the problem was not some mysterious malign influence from the tree, but the action of mosquitoes who favoured the damp and boggy conditions where the trees thrived in dense patches of woodland.

There was a correlation between the presence of the fever tree in large numbers and the prevalence of malaria, but no causal relationship.

As the example in Box 1.2 suggests, it is all too easy to jump to conclusions about apparently simple explanations of what can be complicated situations. As a result we can take inappropriate and wasteful action, whether this consists of cutting down trees unnecessarily or, in business and organisational contexts, implementing changes that might actually make a bad situation worse. As critical thinkers we need to combine the need to act decisively with a cautious approach to the evidence. A good starting point is to be aware of what patterns there may be in the available data and what they reveal about the current situation and potential future trends.

Activity 1.1: Patterns in data

Allow **5 minutes** for this activity.

Purpose: to understand the differences between a number of generic patterns in data

Both time-series and explanatory forecasting present the user with data in which patterns may be discernible. With time-series forecasting, the challenge for forecasters is to discover the real patterns (if any). For a moment, think of a set of data such as monthly ice cream sales over three years in a particular region. What kind of patterns might you expect to see in the monthly figures over time? Make a note of your answer before moving on to the Discussion.

Discussion

Certainly you might expect to see a seasonal pattern, with sales going up and down at different parts of the year. Seasonal patterns repeat themselves with predictable regularity within particular timescales. You might also expect to see, over the longer term, evidence of a trend as overall consumption either goes up or down over time. This is quite a common phenomenon in many consumer products and services, reflecting changes in consumer needs and ways to satisfy them. A further pattern might also reveal itself, even within an overall trend – that of the cycle. Cycles differ from trends insofar as they go up and down, whereas trends move in one direction only.

They are also different from seasonal patterns, as cycles have less regular time spans. Of course, it is also just possible that the data might show very little variation from one period to another – in which case you could describe the pattern as horizontal (i.e. flat). And finally, you would expect to see some fluctuations which did not fit into either seasonal, trend, cyclical or horizontal patterns – just random variations (or 'error' as forecasters tend to call it).

Time-series forecasting

For time-series forecasting, the challenge is to analyse the data in search of internal relationships between the figures, which might give a clue to what we could reasonably expect to continue into the future.

For example, ice cream monthly sales figures might reveal movements from month to month. Across a whole year a seasonal pattern might emerge, with peak sales in summer. But how could you spot a longer term trend? You might gather more data – say for three years instead of one. You could allow for a seasonal pattern when assessing the figures but what about fluctuations between months caused by short-term conditions (such as freak weather)? How can you see past the monthly figures to the longer term? One way is to calculate moving annual totals. To do so, you need to group the data into 12-month periods ending on successive months, and calculate the totals for each set of 12 months in sequence. Obviously, from a set of monthly data for three years you would only be able to calculate 25 such moving annual totals (the first being at the end of the first 12 months of data). But that might be enough to alert you to an underlying trend, and allow you to forecast more confidently.

Looking at data in this way has what is known as a 'smoothing' effect, because it evens out short-term fluctuations to minimise the effects of error (i.e. random movements) in the data, and reveals genuine long-term trends.

Activity 1.2 gives you a chance to see how this works in practice, and what potential insight it might offer you from a set of figures.

Activity 1.2: Smoother ice cream

This activity should take **30 minutes** if you do it using a computer spreadsheet programme, considerably longer if you do it by hand (and calculator).

Purpose: to practise the simple analysis and interpretation of basic quantitative data

Important: The most convenient way to do this exercise is to use the spreadsheet on the module website (select the link to extra resources in the Block 6 section of the Study planner). Using a spreadsheet programme like Microsoft Excel, you can automate the performance of the calculations and graphing involved. If you do not use Microsoft Excel, we have provided a link to the data, which you can then copy and paste into an alternative spreadsheet programme. If you are not sufficiently familiar with functions like 'Insert > Chart' or whatever your spreadsheet package calls its facility to produce graphs, use the 'Help' facility provided as part of the software package.

Table 1.1 is a set of data representing ice cream sales from Gelati, a hypothetical family-owned company based in a UK seaside town.

Calculate moving annual totals for the years ending December Year 1, January Year 2, February Year 2 and so on until December Year 3. So, for example, the moving annual total for the year ending December of Year 1 is 1230, for January of Year 2 it is 1232, and so on. This will result in 25 figures, each representing the last 12 months' sales on a rolling basis over two years and one month. What, if any, patterns emerge? What does looking at the moving annual total tell you that looking at the monthly data doesn't? Hint: graphing the data can be helpful.

Table 1.1: Gelati ice cream monthly sales over three years

Month	Year 1 (000 litres)	Year 2 (000 litres)	Year 3 (000 litres)
January	36	38	30
February	37	64	34
March	49	50	52
April	73	90	80
May	111	121	115
June	197	192	181
July	234	217	201
August	235	204	220
September	123	102	103
October	49	76	64
November	37	51	56
December	49	64	66

Discussion

My calculations are given in Table 1.2.

Table 1.2: Gelati ice cream sales: moving annual totals

Month and year	Moving 12-monthly totals
December Y1	1230
January Y2	1232
February Y2	1259
March Y2	1260
April Y2	1277
May Y2	1287
June Y2	1282
July Y2	1265
August Y2	1234
September Y2	1213
October Y2	1240

November Y2	1254
December Y2	1269
January Y3	1261
February Y3	1231
March Y3	1233
April Y3	1223
May Y3	1217
June Y3	1206
July Y3	1190
August Y3	1206
September Y3	1207
October Y3	1195
November Y3	1200
December Y3	1202

My resulting graph is given in Figure 1.1.

A clear pattern of seasonality emerges, accompanied by an overall trend downwards in sales. You could argue that the trend is so slight as not to cause undue alarm, but if you were basing sales forecasts on this graph for the next year or the year after, you would need to take it into account.

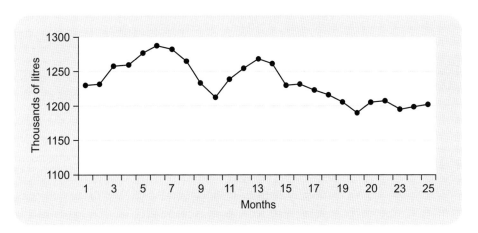

Figure 1.1: Moving annual total ice cream sales for Gelati over 25 months (Month 1 = December Year 1)

Looking at just the raw monthly sales figures for each of the 25 months shown in Table 1.1 reveals the pattern in Figure 1.2 when graphed.

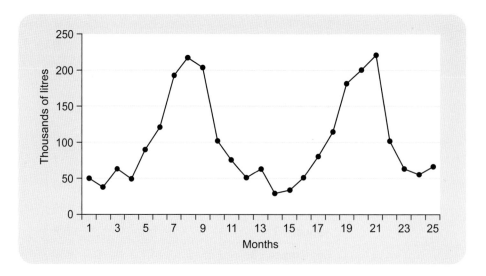

Figure 1.2: Monthly sales from December Y1 to December Y3 for Gelati (Month 1 = December Year 1)

Here you might be tempted to believe that months 23, 24 and 25 show a recovery in sales, which is likely to extend into the future. You could imagine the company board looking at the graph and thinking, 'We have turned the corner.' But this is not borne out by the long-term trend revealed by the smoothing process of using a moving annual total in Figure 1.1. Of course, judgement still plays an important role in how a manager interprets figures such as these. The importance of statistical analysis is to clarify what the data might be saying, but the final responsibility lies with the user to make sense of the story.

Explanatory forecasting

Now let us turn to explanatory forecasting – the other form of quantitative forecasting dealt with by Makridakis et al. (1998). When you were thinking earlier in Activity 1.1 about what kinds of patterns might emerge from sales data, did you speculate as to why the figures might vary? Apart from the unlikely pattern of horizontal data, we discussed seasonality, trends and cycles. For ice cream, seasonality can be explained by the weather – in hotter months ice cream is more appealing than when there is frost on the ground. As to a potential long-term trend of declining consumption, perhaps you speculated that many people's adoption of healthier lifestyles may be bad news for manufacturers of foods that are high in fat and sugar (ice cream included). And perhaps we could explain the cyclical pattern by reference to the way in which the general economy moves. When the economy is prospering, people have more disposable income and might be more prepared to spend it on treats like ice cream. We know that the economy moves in cycles, but that their duration and magnitude are not readily predictable. Relative unpredictability is, in fact, the main thing that differentiates cyclical from seasonal data – although some economists argue that economic cycles do show some regularity, as suggested in Box 1.3.

Box 1.3: Waving goodbye

Nikolai Kondratieff (1892–1938) was one of the economic brains driving the post-revolution Soviet economy. An architect of the original five-year plan, he developed a theory about long-term business cycles using data going back as far as 1789, which continues to influence contemporary thinking about the future. In 1925, he published results arguing that prices had risen steadily for 25 years to a high point in 1815, and then gradually declined for the next 35 years – the first of a series of 'Kondratieff waves', which have continued through subsequent history. Many other economists have supported this view, contending that technological, scientific or economic upheavals instigate cycles, which take from ten to 60 years to complete. The theory is of intense interest to investors, as it offers some guidance as to when they might expect to catch an upward trend in a market. The good news is that (in spite of the global economic crisis of 2007–8) a generally positive trend should be emerging in the first quarter of the twenty-first century as the long-term downward effects of the 1973 oil crisis finally play out. The bad news is that some of us will not be around to reap the benefits by the time they arrive. Kondratieff himself came to a sad end, executed in 1938 after seven years in a labour camp having disagreed with Stalin's disastrous total collectivisation of agriculture.

The key idea with explanatory forecasting is to identify the relationship between one or more independent variable(s) like the weather, or slimming club membership statistics, or perceived economic security, and a dependent variable like ice cream sales, in a way which will support future predictions of the behaviour of the dependent variable (also known as the 'forecast' variable). As we have said earlier, we are looking for a correlation. Proving a direct cause is a lot more problematic, but there has to be some kind of explanatory logic linking the independent to the dependent variable. Thinking again about ice cream sales, what are the independent variables that might affect the dependent variable of sales in this market? We have already mentioned weather, adoption rates of healthy lifestyles, and people's sense of their economic security (the elusive 'feel-good factor' so beloved of politicians in the UK). What other variables might come into play? Distribution (i.e. how and where products and services are available) is an important one in the ice cream market, and has led to 'freezer wars' in the past, where manufacturers would make frozen storage units available to retailers only on condition that they did not carry competitor products. The more outlets that carry your brand, the greater access you have to customers. Pricing might be another important variable affecting sales, and levels of advertising and promotional support will also feature in any list of factors relevant to sales.

From observation and experiment, it might be possible to work out the relative importance of each of these factors (or at least the most important ones) with sufficient confidence to combine them into a model which seeks to explain the dependent variable of ice cream sales. You might even be able to get away with relying on just one independent variable in the model, if you could be confident of the strength of its correlation with the forecast variable. So, for example, if you were able to determine that the weather was far and away the most important influence on ice cream sales, you could predict your sales volumes using what you know about weather patterns (though the accuracy of your sales forecast would, of course, depend on the accuracy of your weather forecast). You might be better off using an independent variable (or set of variables) of whose future value you can be more sure – such as levels of advertising or distribution support, over which you have some control. Naturally, you would also have to have a good idea of their correlation to sales from past data.

This process of modelling a dependent (forecast) variable as a function of a set of one or more independent (explanatory) variable(s) is known as regression. If you have only one independent variable in your model, this is known as simple regression. If, as may be more likely, you are using more than one independent variable, it is known as multiple regression. The term 'regression' itself seems rather an odd word to describe something that is concerned with plotting a trend into the future. The use of the term is to do with history. Sir Francis Galton (1822–1911), the British geneticist and explorer, discovered a phenomenon he called 'regression towards the mean'. Seeking to establish how children inherited traits from their parents, he found that very tall or short fathers tended to have sons who were, respectively, shorter or taller than themselves, thus nearer to average height. Galton called this phenomenon 'regression towards the mean' because the next generation 'regressed' towards the average ('mean') height of the population, and he developed regression analysis as a statistical technique to analyse it. So, even though it refers to a technique used in search of the future, 'regression' as a term has stuck.

Whatever the history of the term, the important thing to take from this account of regression is that it is a rational, quantitative technique, which relies on the future continuation of patterns that have been observed or established in the past. This is fine in circumstances where the relationships underpinning such patterns remain stable. But – as we have seen in Block 2's account of dynamic environments – stability is not a characteristic that organisations can count on. First, the turbulent nature of social, technological, economic and political change can muddy the waters to the point where previously reliable indicators become misleading, or at least a good deal less useful than they have been. Second, as we will see in our discussion of complexity theory in Unit 2, the notion of independent and dependent variables may misrepresent, or at least oversimplify, the way in which all parts of a system are interdependent.

The implication is that, while quantitative forecasting can be very useful in the short to medium term, it is less helpful when looking at the longer term. Yet the far horizon is precisely where an organisation's strategic thinking needs to aim, or it will get distracted by the 'day-to-day'. Thinking back to Block 1 you may remember the four types of decision categorised by Ansoff (1987). These ranged from operational decisions, through programme and policy decisions, to strategic decisions. As you will recall, the respective timescales of the consequences of such decisions range from the day-to-day for operational decisions, through months and years for programme and policy decisions, to what can be many years in the case of strategic decisions with long-term consequences. The usefulness of quantitative forecasting, because of its reliance on established patterns repeating themselves in the future, tends to be limited to shorter- and medium-term timescales. By definition, therefore, it has limited use in the longer-term timescales associated with strategic decision making.

1.3: Qualitative forecasting methods

Qualitative forecasting uses non-numerical data, such as interviews, news media content, written reports and visual information. Makridakis et al. sound a note of caution about qualitative forecasting, but acknowledge its contribution in the appropriate circumstances, associating it with longer term strategic uses:

> It is more difficult to measure the usefulness of qualitative forecasts [than of quantitative ones]. They are used mainly to provide hints, to aid the planner, and to supplement quantitative forecasts, rather than to provide a specific numerical forecast. Because of their nature and cost, they are used almost exclusively for medium- and long-range situations such as formulating strategy, developing new products and technologies, and developing long-range plans. Although doubts are often expressed about the value of qualitative forecasting, it frequently provides useful information for managers … Qualitative methods can be used successfully in conjunction with quantitative methods in such areas as product development, capital expenditures, goal and strategy formation, and mergers, by even medium and small organisations. Whatever the shortcomings of qualitative methods, frequently the only alternative is no forecast at all.

(1998, p. 12)

This slightly grudging comparison of qualitative with quantitative methods is perhaps a little unfair. While both forms of forecasting are complementary in how their results may be applied, the notions of statistical reliability on which quantitative methods draw are simply not available to qualitative forecasting because it does not use numerical data. Instead, qualitative forecasting draws on data such as accumulated knowledge or expertise, which tend to be vested in individuals. This can be accessed through reports or publications – for example, the kind of sources that organisations might use for ongoing environmental analysis. Specific forecasting tasks may simply involve asking an expert for his or her view on future developments in a particular field. An individual forecast is, of course, inevitably a personal judgement. However, it is possible to compensate for personal bias and limited viewpoints by using multiple participants. The interactions within a group of people engaged on a forecasting task are likely to produce richer outputs than those created by individuals on their own – making a wider range of perspectives and ideas available to each member.

Jury method

This brings together a group of experts (and/or managers) in order to compare their individual forecasts. Through discussion and negotiation of these potentially disparate accounts of the future, the group agrees an overall corporate forecast. Debate and discussion can help to make assumptions visible and open to question, and expose possibilities which would not become apparent to individuals on their own. However, like any situation in which an 'in-group' can form, the jury method runs the risk of 'groupthink' – the term coined by the North American psychologist, Irving Janis (1972) to describe how a group of otherwise highly intelligent and resourceful people can develop complacent overconfidence in their decisions and conclusions. 'According to the groupthink hypothesis, members of any small cohesive group tend to maintain esprit de corps by unconsciously developing a number of shared illusions and related norms that interfere with critical thinking and reality testing' (Janis, 1982, p. 35). The results for forecasting might include reluctance to face up to adverse or challenging possibilities, or a failure to articulate ideas that others might dismiss as far-fetched or perverse. Forecasts, as we have observed, need to be neutral and unbiased. Group-based forecasting needs to be vigilant for signs of groupthink, and encourage positive challenge, criticality and respect for the ideas that emerge.

Activity 1.3: Avoiding groupthink

Allow **10 minutes** for this activity.

Purpose: to relate the phenomenon of groupthink to your personal experience

Consider a situation (professional, personal or in a study context) where the outcome of a group process, such as a discussion or meeting, could have been better had it not been for groupthink. List some of the ways in which the problem could have been avoided.

Discussion

Your response to this activity will depend on the particular situation you chose to consider, but it's likely that your list of ways to avoid groupthink will contain at least some of the ideas listed in this discussion. My situation is a tutorial, where a group working on a short case study was 'taken over' by a particularly keen member. The resulting discussion soon became limited to refining his view of the case. The group appeared to finish their work very quickly compared to the other groups in the room and could not understand why everyone else was taking such a long time (in fact, they began to show signs of mild impatience). In the plenary session that followed, it emerged that they had missed a whole aspect of the case, which the other groups had developed and learned from.

As to ways of avoiding this problem, in retrospect I wish I had noticed sooner what was going on and intervened. A better solution would have been to introduce the activity by emphasising the importance of everyone making a contribution – and by legitimating respectful dissent and challenge in the discussion. Alternatively, I could have designed the activity more robustly, by preceding the discussion with a period of silent re-reading of the material where participants had to make independent notes on their view of the case. Or, I could have asked each group to appoint a chair, one of whose responsibilities was to make sure that everyone contributed to the discussion. Preparation, structure and organisation are each ways of improving group outcomes.

1.4: Scenario planning

Scenario planning sets out to create plausible, but contrasting, versions of the future. It is a controversial methodology because it deliberately encourages the creation of what are called robust strategies. The entire thrust of the process of analysis, choice and implementation, which we have been studying in this module, aims to produce optimal strategy (i.e. the best strategy for an expected set of circumstances). Because scenario planning looks at a range of different but plausible futures, it cannot point to a single expected set of circumstances (unless scenarios are graded by probability – an issue to which we will return) and so the idea of optimal strategy becomes irrelevant. In its place, scenario planning develops robust strategy that will withstand a range of potential sets of circumstances – so that the organisation will survive in multiple scenarios and, ideally, prosper in a few. In conditions of environmental turbulence this may be a much more realistic option than recommendations based on conventional planning.

As well as being controversial, scenario planning can make substantial demands on an organisation. Roxburgh (2009) points out: 'Scenarios are in fact harder than they look – harder to conceptualise, harder to build and uncomfortably rich in shortcomings. A good one takes time to build, and so a whole set takes a correspondingly larger investment of time and energy'. Verity in Reading 17 (see Activity 1.4) suggests that its very flexibility as a technique (and the resulting difficulty of clear definition and description) may act as a barrier to the adoption of scenario planning as an approach. However she also underlines its many potential benefits.

Activity 1.4: Reading 'Scenario planning as a strategy technique'

Please allow **120 minutes** for this activity.

Purpose: to establish an understanding of the uses and limitations of scenario planning from Reading 17, 'Scenario planning as a strategy technique' by Julie Verity

Please read the article with the following questions in mind. When you have finished, first make brief notes in answer to the questions, then review your answers against the Discussion provided for this activity.

1   Why is scenario planning not more widely used?

2   Why do we use the term 'scenario'?

3   According to Schwartz (1991) what is the end result of scenario planning?

4 What are the two main styles of scenario planning discussed in the article?

5 Explain the conflict of opinion about whether scenarios should be used for exploration or decision support.

6 The article states several times that scenario planning is flexible. List some ways in which scenarios can differ from each other.

Discussion

1 It's difficult to ascertain the true extent of the use of scenario planning in organisations because of commercial confidentiality. The very flexibility of the technique makes it difficult to describe and define, and there are differences in opinion about how scenarios should be developed and used. Managers don't like to admit uncertainty about the future (given the need to show confidence as a leader). Indeed, a need to feel confident about the future has been argued to be an evolutionary trait in humans. Large-scale scenario planning is expensive and time-consuming, deterring smaller organisations and restricting the frequency of use for larger organisations. Cultural norms may also interfere with the effectiveness of the process.

2 The name comes from the Hollywood term for the story of a film, and has stuck because of the importance of narrative in scenarios.

3 Schwartz (1991) argues scenario planning results in better decisions about the future from deeper understanding of the forces shaping future events.

4 The two main styles are 'intuitive' and 'formal'. Intuitive scenario planning was developed by the Stanford Research Institute (SRI) and Shell. It concentrates on stories and qualitative input, and aims to challenge mental maps. Formal scenario planning had similar origins, but was developed at the University of Southern California. It relies on quantitative inputs to create computer-generated scenarios against which strategies are tested. A third school of scenario planning using trend-impact analysis is also mentioned. Verity suggests that it is impossible to make hard and fast distinctions between the styles as intuitive scenarios can involve quantitative inputs and are deemed credible by their developers, and formal scenarios still require an element of qualitative judgement.

5 Proponents of intuitive scenario planning point to learning as the most important outcome and emphasise process, whereas decision-support advocates see the proper use of scenario planning as applying its product (the scenarios themselves) to potential strategies to test their ability to withstand future circumstances. For decision-support applications, it makes sense to judge which scenarios are most likely to occur (as they will be most relevant to the success of a potential strategy). The very idea of grading scenarios by probability is, according to the intuitive school of thought, a contradiction in terms. They are not meant to be forecasts of more or less likelihood, but a set of plausible futures encompassing a range of probable and improbable circumstances. Rather than testing strategy against the most probable ones, all should be used. History shows that improbable things do happen, and can have an enormous

effect. To downplay the improbable is to lose the point of scenario planning according to this view.

6   Scenarios can be differentiated from each other by how long or short term they are, at what level they are created (e.g. global, national, industry, firm, market), how much uncertainty is included, and what their scope is (e.g. they can be broad, or restricted to exploring how an individual product will perform under a series of alternative conditions). Different levels of scenario can be used to complement each other.

The advantages of scenario planning

As Verity argues in Reading 17, the uses of scenario planning for exploration and decision support are not mutually exclusive (with the proviso that using scenarios for decision support does not lead to an undue emphasis on their relative probability). Here we want to develop your understanding of the uses to which scenario planning can be put.

> By considering multiple scenarios at the same time, the organisation can keep from being locked into one view of the future while sharing a common set of frameworks for discovering new signals.
>
> Where organisations normally filter out weak signals from the periphery especially those that don't fit the dominant world view, scenario planning systematises the hunt for weak signals that may foreshadow fundamental shifts in the marketplace and society at large. Rather than muffling weak signals, scenarios can magnify 'postcards from the edge' so that they are visible to many more eyes.
>
> (Day and Schoemaker, 2006, p. 95)

Day and Schoemaker emphasise how scenario planning can sensitise managers to small but potentially important changes in the environment ('weak signals'), which a more monolithic view of the future might exclude from their notice. Weak signals often herald the beginning of something important, so the earlier the organisation can start noticing them the longer it has to decide what to do about them. Our existing mental maps can prevent us understanding environmental change. We all tend to make sense of the world from what we know of it – shaped by our social and cultural background, education and experience. This can work well in many situations – but it imposes limits on our ability to envisage the unexpected, and thus to cope with it when it happens. In organisations with strong cultures, members are socialised into particular mental maps. Day and Schoemaker (2006) claim that scenario planning can render this paradigm more flexible, and better at detecting change, by providing a common set of frameworks which accommodate uncertainty.

Another way of describing the realignment of mental maps is to call it 'learning'. Learning involves abandoning outmoded or no-longer useful perspectives in favour of more comprehensive ones, and it is as important to organisations trying to improve their strategic thinking as it is to individuals studying for a degree. Learning from what works and what doesn't is how organisational culture develops (Schein, 2004). You may have noticed in the course of your studies that your views on particular issues and interpretation of the world in general have changed – perhaps directly as a result of particular experiences, or more gradually as a result of developing new habits of thought. The same thing happens on an organisational scale in response to new stimuli over time. In a classic article about the use of scenarios to foster organisational learning, the Dutch management scholars Robert Bood and Theo Postma summarise a number of questions (which by now may have a familiar ring to you) about the ability of managers to devise and implement deliberate, rational strategy given the image of reality their mental maps produce:

> Above all, as ordinary human beings, managers are not the rational, all-overlooking actors some strategic management theorists wanted us to believe for a long time. Managers often do not devise and explore strategic problems properly and do not systematically generate alternatives. Instead they only partially study one or two alternatives that either are readily available or already favoured for a long time. After they have made a choice, they often stick firmly to their initial choices even if altered circumstances require modifications. Last, but not least, they base their interpretation of the outcome on its desirability. Being ordinary people, managers work within cognitive limits.
>
> Whether we like it or not we are all severely constrained in our possibilities to cope adequately with the host of different stimuli and data we are confronted with daily. Cognitive psychology teaches us that, in order to be able to act, people construe simplified mental images of the world they live in and impose these images upon the world around them. These images function as a frame of reference for action and interpretation of the world and the data it produces. The images are the world as seen through our eyes. General ways in which people cognitively simplify stimuli and data are well-known as heuristics or rules of thumb. Examples include 'wishful thinking', 'availability' and 'selective perception'.
>
> (Bood and Postma, 1997, pp. 636–7)

Stretching managers' mental maps so that they abandon such rules of thumb to explore the unfamiliar and ask 'what if?' is one of six benefits of scenario planning which Bood and Postma list. The other five are:

- Evaluating and selecting strategies – providing a framework of future possibilities against which to test possible strategies. As we will see, this promotes flexible, 'robust' strategies rather than the more precise ones we tend to associate with shorter-term strategic horizons assuming relatively stable conditions.

- Integrating data – scenarios can integrate both qualitative and quantitative data, and incorporate data from other forecasting techniques. They bring together different sources of knowledge in organisations in a convenient forum.

- Exploring the future – thinking into the long term encourages managers to debate causal processes (however difficult these may be to specify with certainty) and to reflect on the important and enduring, rather than the urgent but relatively transitory, issues which preoccupy them for most of their working lives.

- Promoting increased awareness of environmental uncertainties – scenario planning encourages managers to accept uncertainty rather than trying to ignore or play it down in the context of more formal planning techniques.

- Triggering and accelerating organisational learning – just as scenario planning has the capacity to integrate existing knowledge in an organisation, so it can act as a focus for learning. Organisations tend to learn from experience, through evaluating what has worked and what hasn't (assuming they survive long enough to do so in the latter case). Scenarios can speed this process up by encouraging managers to develop and test ideas about the future.

Bood and Postma's advocacy of the organisational learning benefits of scenario planning is typical of the 'intuitive' school of scenario planning, which emphasises the learning value of the process, as much as the scenarios themselves. The process aspects of scenario planning can also provide a way of promoting learning and communication breakthroughs between, rather than within, organisations, as illustrated in Activity 1.5.

Activity 1.5: Strategic conversation

Allow **10 minutes** for this activity.

Purpose: to exemplify the use of scenario planning in a public policy context to promote mutual understanding between interest groups

Please access the module website to watch the clip that forms the basis of this activity, 'Creative thinking under siege' from Sophia Tickell of SustainAbility (Tickell, 2009).

As you watch the clip, consider how scenario planning helped the Pharma Futures project to break the deadlock between the industry representatives and the investors.

There is a transcript of the clip on the website, should you need to refer to it.

Discussion

Sophia Tickell describes a situation where industry and investors appeared to be stuck in their own mental maps of the world, and consequently locked in mutual distrust and misunderstanding. Participating in scenario planning led them to reframe their respective positions by bringing their assumptions to the surface and allowing them to be challenged.

The process of scenario planning

Up to this point, we have talked about the nature and benefits of scenario planning but how do organisations actually go about doing it? The actual mechanics of the process are relatively straightforward in theory, but can become quite demanding of time and resources in practice. Furthermore, as different organisations and consultancies have taken up the technique, it has developed in different ways. In Reading 17, Verity describes how some consultants are more committed to a strategy-testing approach, and others more committed to organisational learning as an outcome (although we should re-emphasise that it is perfectly possible to enjoy both benefits at the same time).

Given the technique's flexibility and the different starting points taken by organisations with differing experience of scenario planning, it is hard to specify a precise process for the technique in the way that, for example, the Delphi technique has developed. There is evidence that the intricate dialogue between planners and managers, which Wack (1985) reported from his experience at Royal Dutch/Shell, has simplified over time (Open University, 2000, p. 192). Furthermore, in spite of the apparent sophistication implied in much of the literature about scenario planning, some of its supporters claim that it can be made much simpler and shorter. However, all scenario planning involves three main phases: inputs from environmental analysis, transformation of these inputs into a number of plausible scenarios, and the output of strategy formulation. As we have seen, this output can include the testing of strategic options against a variety of scenarios to gauge how well they would stand up in different circumstances. As we have already observed, such strategies are known as 'robust' strategies, because they are capable of withstanding a number of different future scenarios.

Drawing on their work as consultants, a group of strategy researchers based at Strathclyde University suggest a sequence of eight steps in creating scenarios (Burt et al., 2006) which we will use to exemplify the process. They centre their account on a case study of a company involved in energy generation whose senior managers were particularly keen on accelerating organisational learning.

Step 1: Identify areas of concern

Any form of forecasting, including scenario planning, requires a focus. What is 'the problem'? Or, to put it another way, what are the particular opportunities and threats that face the organisation in its current environment? The STEP framework, or one of its variants, can provide a comprehensive structure for this question. Managers are likely to be all too familiar with the main themes here – but this is the starting point for the next stage, which asks them to begin to confront the unfamiliar.

Step 2: Brainstorm for key uncertainties

Revisiting the areas of interest from Step 1, the participants now brainstorm factors likely to impact on their organisation's strategy in whatever timeframe they have chosen to explore. Doing this within a longer-term perspective is unsettling, but helps reveal which aspects of the environment are relatively predictable, and which are simply unknown. It's important to realise this distinction, as it is at the heart of how the scenario-planning process develops from this step forward. Relatively predictable trends (what Donald Rumsfeld might term 'known unknowns', see Box 1.4) are things like demographic change, the declining cost of telecoms, increased globalisation and deregulation. The precise effects and timings of established trends such as these are difficult to gauge, but we can factor them into our plans with confidence. On the other hand, there are plenty of things that will happen in the future, but about which we cannot know in advance: the 'unknown unknowns'. Such key uncertainties might include technology breakthroughs, which create rapidly expanding new markets for goods and services and destabilise existing market structures, or the unheralded entry of a new competitor into an established market. Such uncertainties have enormous power to affect strategy. Participants need to engage in informed speculation about what might happen in order to surface such destabilising possibilities.

Box 1.4: In the know?

As we know, there are known knowns. There are things we know we know. We also know there are known unknowns. That is to say we know there are some things we do not know. But there are also unknown unknowns, the ones we don't know we don't know.

(Source: Rumsfeld, 2002)

Step 3: Cluster key uncertainties

On their own, the uncertainties exposed in Step 2 may not move organisational learning on very far. However, placing them in related clusters begins to develop a sense of how things might be linked causally and logically in change relationships. Burt et al. (2006, p. 64) illustrate this with a group of uncertainties brainstormed by their energy generation company such as 'economic decline or growth and its impact on power', 'US involvement with Europe in trade relations' or 'world population too many or too few'. The participants cluster these under the heading of 'Global economy'. By combining these factors in a cluster and giving it this name, the group is demonstrating consensus about the importance of this set of issues. The discussion involved reveals and challenges individual assumptions. Clustering, in particular, forces participants to make connections and see implications, which up to this point may have eluded them. This is an example of how mental maps shift and rearrange themselves in the scenario-generation process, producing the potential change in perspective so valued by Wack (1985) and argued by Day and Schoemaker (2006) to be an essential benefit of the technique.

Step 4: Prioritise uncertainties: the 'importance/uncertainty' matrix

One of the problems about environmental analysis is the sheer volume of potentially significant material it generates. Managers face the daunting task of discerning which issues and information deserve their attention, and which are just 'noise'. The early stages of scenario planning can be similarly confusing, so Step 4 is an opportunity to do some prioritisation. Visual representations are useful in developing strategy (think of all the matrices and diagrams, which populate strategy textbooks). Step 4 accordingly uses a visual tool, the 'importance/uncertainty' matrix, to sort out the key issues to be taken further in the process.

Plotting high predictability (certainty) to low predictability of outcome (uncertainty) on the y axis, and low impact (unimportance) to high impact (importance) on the x axis, the matrix allows participants to assign clusters to quadrants based on their perceived predictability and impact. Figure 1.3 shows such a matrix for our energy generation company. You will note that 'Global economy', the cluster we mentioned in Step 3, is considered both unpredictable and of high impact. Its uncertainty combined with its importance mark it out (along with the other cluster occupying this quadrant) as something with the potential to drive major change, and influence the future in unforeseen ways. Again the discussion and reasoning participants undertake to prioritise uncertainties is a valuable source of learning.

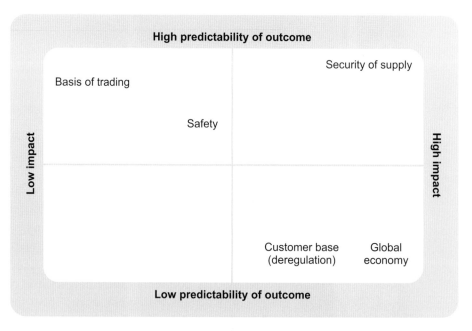

Figure 1.3: Importance/uncertainty matrix from an energy generation company's scenario planning process

From Figure 1.3, it is clear that the two most significant clusters as arranged by participants were the changing nature of the customer base and the shape of the global economy. Therefore, these were the overriding themes that were taken into the next stage, forming the essential basis for the scenarios which followed.

Step 5: Develop scenarios

One of the challenges facing participants in scenario planning is that we tend to be naturally dualistic in our attitudes to the future. In other words, we tend to see things as either good or bad. The popularity of the phrase 'worst-case scenario' is a case in point. The point of generating multiple scenarios about the future is not to offer a 'best-case' and 'worst-case' estimate. Instead it is about exploring the plausible extremes to which the chosen clusters might develop, in other words the 'limits of possibility' for where these clusters might end up in the future. So, in the case we are using to illustrate the process, discussion and analysis led to the conclusion that the two chosen clusters might turn out between two extremes of a continuum in each case as follows:

(a) Changes in the global economy – on a continuum between harmony among nations, leading to growth and increasing demand for energy at one end, and conflict resulting in fragmentation and sluggish demand at the other.

(b) Changes in the customer base – on a continuum between large numbers of geographically dispersed customers with different needs at one end, and a few very large customers wielding enormous purchasing power at the other.

Again, the popular visual tool of a two-by-two matrix comes in useful to illustrate how this works (as we shall see in Activity 1.6) and how it leads to four alternative views of the future. These were given memorable titles. Anything you can do to make decision-makers pay attention to your scenarios is a bonus – snappy titles that sum up the gist of the scenario are a very good idea in this respect.

Activity 1.6: Slotting in scenarios

Allow **10 minutes** for this activity.

Purpose: to consolidate your understanding of scenario development

Here are brief descriptions of the basic scenarios, which the power generation company managers came up with in Step 5. Slot their titles into the matrix below, each in its appropriate quadrant.

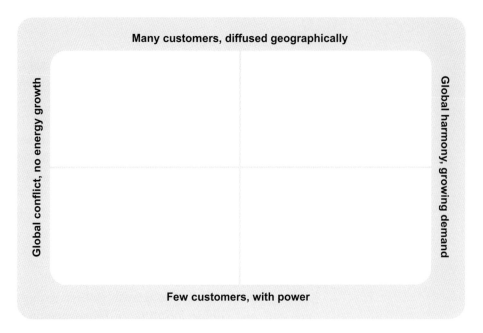

Retrenchment

Increased terrorism has dampened business activity, reduced travel and cut international trade. Falling demand for energy has led to fewer new generating facilities, and less research and development. There is increased focus on existing customers, and little prospect for growth.

Fill your boots

This informal expression means 'take as much as you want' – perhaps because after you've filled your pockets your boots are the next most convenient receptacle. This scenario sees an expanding world economy benefitting from deregulation and international development. Growth means increased demand for power, more expensive labour, and problems about supply leading to attempts to widen available sources. Nuclear power, however, continues to be regarded with unease, meaning that conventional generators make lots of money.

Survive or bust

Increased conflict results in falling levels of international trade and more regionalisation. Confidence levels are low. Stock markets are dominated by short-term asset-stripping (with many companies going bankrupt) and takeover activity by surviving companies determined to reap economies of scale. In turn, bigger customers demand lower energy prices, and margins shrink. In the face of international protectionism and stalled demand the game becomes one of survival.

Win or lose

Global economic growth spurs increased demand for energy, which is largely satisfied by alternative supplies. An expanding European Union (EU) increases access to potential customers. Several large players emerge in the generating business due to mergers and acquisitions; resulting in just two or three 'super generator' companies competing in the European market. EU funding and competition policy is concentrated towards helping new member state economies rather than monitoring the expansion of generating facilities.

Discussion

Your matrix should look like Figure 1.4.

Figure 1.4: Completed 'Energy Generation Futures' scenario grid for Activity 1.6

Step 6: Articulate and flesh out scenarios

The participants take the very basic scenarios from Step 5, such as those which emerge from the two-by-two matrix, and develop a fuller 'storyline' for each. Some of the additional detail from this step is incorporated in the very brief scenario outlined in Activity 1.6 (for example, the role and behaviour of the EU as an actor and regulator became an important element in some of the scenarios). Thinking through the likely sequence of events that produce the end-state of each scenario helps to suggest relevant details. By using their imagination to 'live in' each scenario, the participants can ensure that their imagined worlds are consistent and internally coherent. For example, in the scenarios that envisage a declining economy, one would not expect there to be high levels of inflation. The linkages between different aspects of a scenario can be explored and their likely effect on other facets of the future gauged.

Step 7: Identify structural insights and potential discontinuities

By engaging in the process of fleshing out the scenarios and exploring the way that the different forces in the clusters might interact to create new and unexpected effects, participants identify relationships between environmental factors that they might otherwise have missed. In particular, they look for potential changes (discontinuities) which may present radical threats or opportunities. In 'Win or lose', for instance, the combination of an expanding EU and a widening of sources of energy supply resulted in a predicted change in EU competition policy – approving the mergers and acquisition activity which resulted in the 'super generators' configuration. In the 'Win or lose' world this had a convincing logic, but would be difficult to reconcile with the EU's current policy, which would see such mergers as anti-competitive and act to limit them.

Step 8: System behaviour

This final step in the scenario-preparation process, at least in the example used here, concerns a further elaboration of the structural insights from the preceding stage. By trying to understand the scenario as a system – emphasising the interconnectedness of its different elements – participants can validate its plausibility. Techniques here include drawing influence diagrams in order to make explicit the forces that bear on particular events or developments over time. We will return to the idea of systems thinking when we look at the concept of complexity as a way of understanding strategy in Unit 2 of this block. Systems thinking helps users get the most out of the scenario-planning process by consolidating their new mental models of how their business environment works, and, by extension, making them more sensitive to how their intended strategies are likely to play out against it over the long term.

As Verity indicates in Reading 17, the process and application of scenario planning is flexible. Box 1.5 provides a further illustration of scenario planning in practice, in this case by a national tourism organisation which combined elements of both 'intuitive' and 'formal' approaches.

Box 1.5: A vision for VisitScotland

VisitScotland is the national tourism organisation (NTO) for Scotland. As well as marketing Scotland to domestic and international visitors, it advises the Scottish government on policy matters relating to tourism. Because tourism as an industry is affected by so many external factors (such as exchange rate fluctuations, economic confidence, and unforeseen events such as terrorism and disease outbreaks) it makes sense to take a long-term view. As an industry that employs almost one in ten of the Scottish population it has to have a robust vision of the future. Hence the adoption of scenario planning by VisitScotland to frame its strategic thinking.

Scenario planning can accommodate a variety of data inputs and development processes. VisitScotland's approach to scenario planning has been threefold:

- It established a scenario-planning group of internal and external stakeholders.

- It carried out extensive environmental scanning across a wide range of sources.

- It used a forecasting model in combination with economic analysis.

The use of a forecasting model appears at first sight to contradict the 'plural futures' ethos of scenario planning. After all, the great strength of scenarios is their avoidance of a single 'right' predicted future in favour of the generation of plural, plausible futures which encourage flexible thinking and managerial insight. To some extent the inclusion of a forecasting model was to fulfil stakeholder expectations of a quantitative dimension to the outputs. Policymakers, in particular, are comfortable with figures. But the use of a quantitative model also encouraged the planners to ensure internal coherence and a tight logical structure to their scenarios – thus addressing the potential objection to scenario planning that it lacks rigour.

The scenario-planning group itself comprised representatives from a number of organisations with an interest in national or international Scottish tourism, selected with the help of an external consultant. The group drew from financial services, hotel groups, national enterprise companies, environmental organisations and whisky companies. The group ran interactive workshops making use of individual and group methods to articulate and express ideas about the future. Individual techniques included cognitive mapping, which consists of plotting the links between ideas in an individual's view of a particular issue. Group processes included the amalgamation of individual input by means of graphic display techniques – where participants' ideas were clustered by a facilitator on a whiteboard to explore and share assumptions and reveal the connections between aspects of the environment as envisaged by the group. Such techniques underline the systematic nature of phenomena – enabling participants to question previously taken-for-granted assumptions. The 'systems workshops' were complemented by seminars and a programme of lectures.

Less interactive than workshops, the seminars and lectures focused on particular issues with visiting experts and invited guests. Topics included current developments in the EU such as enlargement, economic support initiatives, and demographic trends which have a bearing on future market conditions for tourism. As well as spreading ideas and information, the seminars and lectures brought VisitScotland staff face to face with a wide range of stakeholders and underlined the strategic importance of the project not only to the organisation itself but to the wider community.

These activities ran in tandem with a programme of environmental scanning, which drew on a variety of sources but aimed to provide a systematic and selective digest of environmental developments relevant to tourism. Strathclyde University helped in identifying and tracking critical uncertainties and change, and VisitScotland established a network of 'remarkable people' (a term coined by Shell International to describe experts who do not have direct connections with a particular industry but whose areas of knowledge are highly relevant to its concerns). The network helped in a number of ways – with specialist advice, market intelligence and as a sounding board for ideas. VisitScotland also put in place a programme of staff training in scenario techniques and their application, drawing on the services of its external consultant.

As well as group work and environmental scanning, VisitScotland's scenario-planning approach used a computer-based econometric model. Common in economics, such models require the input of real data and rely on a set of equations, which combines the data according to the estimated relationships between a large number of variables (for example, prices, inflation and exchange rates, likely market sizes and so forth) to predict the effects of different circumstances on tourism volume and spend. Unusually for such a model (but characteristically for scenario planning) the inputs to the model included the impact of shocks (unforeseen environmental developments, such as human or animal epidemics) and changes in policy (such as sudden tax increases). In spite of their sophistication, econometric models based on past data have a tendency to reproduce known trends into the future. The deliberate inclusion of 'shocks' helped counteract this limitation. The fact that this particular model was accessible via a user-friendly computer interface boosted its acceptance by participants as part of their approach to generating and testing different futures.

Dr Ian Yeoman, the VisitScotland lead on scenario planning, emphasises that it needs to be seen as a process rather than a panacea. The work that started in 2005 aims to support the organisation's progress towards 2025 (with an interim goal of increasing tourism revenues by 50 per cent in the first ten years). He comments that: 'Scenario planning is a process, not an answer. You have to make a connection between scenario planning and your organisation. This means showing how the world shapes tourism, not the other way round'.

(Source: adapted from Yeoman and McMahon-Beattie, 2005)

Scenarios and strategy

The preceding subsection and Box 1.5 illustrate the scenario-planning process up to the point of producing and refining the actual scenarios. As we have indicated, some influential proponents of scenario planning see the process itself as the main source of benefit from organisational learning and development. However, the question remains of how to integrate the results into the strategy process. Roxburgh (2009) warns of the danger of paralysis in the face of multiple futures – managers still need to have, and to communicate, a way forward. He suggests that sensitivity to the range of possibilities facing an organisation encourages realism in setting and communicating goals which can enhance rather than undermine the credibility of leaders.

The formal school of scenario planning emphasises its use in testing potential strategies. Lempert et al. (2006) suggest that with sufficient iterations between computer-generated scenarios and lists of strategic options, robust strategies can be chosen with some precision – extending the use of scenario planning into strategic decision making. Ramirez and van der Heijden (2007, p. 97) are more aligned to the intuitive approach, using the analogy of 'wind-tunnelling' to evoke strategy testing within a set of dynamic scenarios. The intuitive approach relies on a limited number of scenarios (between two and four) with clearly demarcated characteristics (and evocative titles) because managers are unlikely to be able to hold more than that number in their minds at any one time. It is, therefore, open to the criticism of lack of rigour but can defend itself on the grounds of comprehensibility.

In Reading 17, Verity points to examples where relatively short-term scenarios have been used to develop new products and services – almost like any other variety of qualitative market research. The point to emphasise, again, is the flexibility of the technique. Our final activity in this unit returns to this theme.

Activity 1.7: Putting scenarios to work

Allow **15 minutes** for this activity.

Purpose: to explore the different uses of scenario planning from a practitioner perspective

Please access the module website to watch the video clip that forms the basis of this activity, 'What to do with the scenarios?' from US consultant and academic Paul Schoemaker (2008). As you watch the clip, make notes on the three main uses he suggests.

There is a transcript of the clip on the website, should you need to refer to it.

Discussion

Schoemaker's first point is that, at a general level, scenarios can be used as lenses for organisational sense-making. He uses a memorable expression about increasing the organisation's 'strategic IQ', whereby organisations learn and become able to engage in dialogue with their stakeholders. His second point is that, at a more operational level, scenarios can help with refining strategy. The virtue of multiple scenarios is in helping avoid inflexible strategy. Finally, at the level of an individual project proposal, scenarios can promote more holistic thinking about risk analysis. He claims that scenario analysis can change the way that companies evaluate their investment proposals, seeing them as a way of buying options on the future.

Summary

This unit has given you an overview of some of the ways in which strategists deal with the issue of the future. We have looked at quantitative and qualitative forecasting and then, at some length, surveyed the technique of scenario planning – identifying intuitive and formal approaches and their respective emphases.

Forecasting in the longer term involves being willing to embrace uncertainty and the implications of a range of possible futures. Uncertainty can be contrasted with the notion of risk in that risk consists of calculable probabilities, whereas uncertainty cannot be quantified. By definition, we can't know the unknowable. But at least we know that it's there in the future waiting for us, so we can do our best to develop our ability to react to emerging circumstances as quickly as possible.

In spite of the lack of widespread adoption reported by Verity in Reading 17, there is evidence that environmental turbulence is attracting companies to re-evaluate the technique. For example, the Danish toymaker Lego announced that it had used scenarios for the first time in 2009 as part of strategy development, precisely in response to the need to develop strategic options to manage uncertainty (*The Economist*, 2009).

Our account of the scenario development process followed an eight-step procedure from Burt et al. (2006):

1 Identify areas of concern

2 Brainstorm for key uncertainties

3 Cluster key uncertainties

4 Prioritise uncertainties: the 'importance/uncertainty' matrix

5 Develop scenarios

6 Articulate and flesh out scenarios

7 Identify structural insights and potential discontinuities

8 System behaviour.

Scenario planning's incorporation into strategy development can range from global use in sense-making, to specific application, to individual projects in the context of risk analysis. The issues of uncertainty, complexity and turbulence, which scenario planning and forecasting highlight in their respective ways, are a very appropriate note to end on, as we move to Unit 2's account of some new ways of understanding strategy – including those drawn from complexity theory.

Unit 2: New understandings of strategy

Aims

In this unit, we survey three contemporary areas of interest for strategy researchers and practitioners: complexity theory, strategy as discourse, and the relationship between strategy and society. Each of these areas of interest departs from what we can call 'orthodox' or traditional strategy approaches. At the same time, there are elements of continuity filling in theoretical gaps or making us pay attention to factors that orthodox strategy looks past.

By the end of this unit, you should be able to:

- describe complexity theory and explain its influence on strategy

- list ways in which complexity thinking complements orthodox approaches to strategy

- link the four bedrock principles identified by Pascale in Reading 18 to strategic management

- explain what is meant by 'the linguistic turn' in social research and its implications for making sense of strategy

- relate the concept of narrative to the practice of strategy

- explain the concepts of power, identity, legitimacy and authority as they relate to strategy

- define the concept of ideology and comment on its relevance to how we make sense of management in general and strategy in particular

- outline the main tenets of critical management studies and corporate social responsibility and take an informed view on their validity with reference to strategy.

2.1: Complexity theory as an approach to strategy

Complexity is a comparatively recent perspective in the strategy literature. It draws on insights from 'complexity science' (which originated in the 1960s as an interdisciplinary approach to understanding complex systems, such as those found in the natural world) and applies them to strategic thinking and strategic management problems. This offers a fresh perspective for strategists nurtured on traditional models of strategy, as the dynamics driving change in complex systems are not the same as those suggested by classical science. In fact, as we will see, complexity theorists offer an understanding of the nature of change itself, which is different from conventional ways of seeing it. You will need to judge for yourself which you find the most plausible.

Perhaps the most well-known complexity researcher in the organisational strategy field is the UK academic Ralph Stacey who began to draw attention to complexity as a perspective on organisation and management during the 1990s. Complexity has also attracted attention from economists, regulators and managers with an interest in developing a better understanding of economic, industry and organisational dynamics. The financial crisis, banking collapses and subsequent recession of 2007–8 accelerated this growing interest because these events highlighted the limitations of the conventional rationality underpinning our traditional economic and strategy models. Prior to 2007, many economists, regulators and managers might have concurred with Professor Robert Lucas, a Nobel-prize-winning economist, when he declared in 2003 that 'the central problem of depression prevention has been solved for all practical purposes' (Krugman, 2008, p. 9). The 2007 global financial crisis proved he was wrong. After the financial crisis emerged, Alan Greenspan, Chairman of the Federal Reserve of the United States from 1987 to 2006, highlighted the inadequacy of models based upon conventional thinking. He pointed out that they had been 'too simple to capture the full array of governing variables that drive economic reality' (Greenspan, 2008). So the question is, what can complexity offer which conventional rational models can not?

At this point it is pertinent to note that complexity is usually portrayed as an alternative paradigm to rational models of strategy. In many ways it is. Complexity theorists do not think in terms of cause and effect, but in terms of interconnections and interdependencies. They seek to understand patterns rather than causes. However, in other ways, complexity can be argued to complement established strategy perspectives in that it addresses issues which are either neglected or ignored in traditional thinking.

Activity 2.1: What complexity adds to our understanding of strategy

This is a continuous activity through your reading of this material on complexity.

Purpose: to help you consolidate your understanding of the complexity perspective as you work through this unit

As you study this material, make a list in your notes of as many ways as strike you in which complexity adds to the understanding provided by the Classical approach to strategy by addressing its limitations.

Discussion

Feedback will be provided in the summary which follows the material on complexity. You will be able to compare your list with the content there.

What is complexity?

Complexity involves a systems approach to the study of the dynamics of environments and organisations. Systems are comprised of a number of connected interdependent parts. A central heating system, for example, consists of a number of interdependent parts such as a boiler, pump, thermostat, radiators and so on. These parts operate together as a system to heat buildings. Central heating systems are comparatively simple mechanical systems in which the relationship between the parts is known. The behaviour of each part is stable. Boilers, pumps and thermostats do not change their behaviour of their own accord. Pumps do not suddenly decide to start heating water. Thermostats do not suddenly decide to start pumping water around the system. The effects of the interacting elements in a central heating system are known and predictable, but other types of system are less predictable. Systems comprised of interacting human beings are a case in point. Central heating systems are closed systems, unaffected by the things that go on around them. Human beings and systems comprised of interacting human beings (such as organisations) are complex systems, open to external influences.

Activity 2.2: Closed or complex systems?

Allow **5 minutes** for this activity.

Purpose: to consider the differences between closed and complex systems

A family is comprised of interacting human beings. It can be conceptualised as a system within which children can grow up and many of the needs of family members can be satisfied. Think about a family as a system. How does this family system differ from a central heating system? Jot down your thoughts.

Discussion

Within a family, the parents and children are interacting agents, but family members do not always behave in the same predictable ways. Families are complex in a way which central heating systems are not. Family members are able to change their behaviour voluntarily. Central heating system components can only behave in the way they are designed to behave. People, on the other hand, can adapt to what they interpret as happening around them by changing their behaviour. Family members can respond to their interactions with each other in more than one way. They are able to change their behaviour when the situation demands. For example, if one partner in a relationship gets upset when the other comes into the house wearing dirty boots, this partner may start taking off the offending boots at the door. The home environment is affected, and can be changed, by the interactions that family members have with each other and other agents with whom they interact in their wider environment. For example, if interactions with the local GP suggest that one or more family member might be overweight, the whole family may start eating more healthy meals.

Consciously or unconsciously, family members both act and react to what others in the family are doing and they also act and react to those with whom they interact outside the family system. These interactions can also impact upon family life.

Family systems are, therefore, more open and complex than central heating systems. Their interactions are not governed by linear cause-and-effect relationships whereby the same stimulus always has the same effect. The agents interacting within the family are adaptive in a way which central heating systems are not. The family can, therefore, be conceptualised as an adaptive system. The thermostat is designed to respond to changes in temperature in only one way and its responses are predetermined. It is unable to decide not to respond to a drop in temperature one day because the family is out and it would be able to save them money on heating bills. It is not adaptive because it cannot change its behaviour when circumstances suggest that this would be beneficial. The thermostat is part of a system consisting of many other interacting components, which can also only respond to change in predetermined ways. Conventional science is concerned with the linear cause-and-effect relationships, which drive change in systems of this type. Complexity science is concerned with non-linear relationships and those properties which make complex systems adaptive.

Activity 2.3: A linear relationship

Allow **1 minute** for this activity.

Purpose: to illuminate the nature of a linear relationship

Think about our central heating system again. What would happen if someone turned up the thermostat?

Discussion

The room or house that was being heated would get hotter. This would be the outcome every time the action of turning up the thermostat was taken. There is a direct linear cause-and-effect relationship between the action of turning up the thermostat and the temperature of the house. In linear relationships, the same stimulus always elicits the same response.

Activity 2.4: A non-linear relationship

Allow **2 minutes** for this activity.

Purpose: to illuminate the nature of a non-linear relationship

Now consider the family. What would happen if a mysterious benefactor made a gift to the family of several thousand pounds?

Discussion

This question is more difficult to answer. The family might spend the money or save it. It might use it to pay off debts. If the family were to be given more than one such gift at different points in time, it would probably do different things with it depending on the circumstances. In other words, the same stimulus (making a gift of several thousand pounds to the family) would have a varying effect. There is a non-linear relationship between this action and the outcome. The same stimulus does not always elicit the same response. Our family will not always behave in the same way when it receives a windfall. Our thermostat, on the other hand, will always respond in the same way to a change in temperature, or being turned up or down.

We are now in a position to answer the question: what is complexity? Complexity is the study of complex adaptive systems in which the dynamics of interaction between the elements or agents are non-linear. Although a family can be conceptualised as a complex adaptive system, those systems in the world of human affairs are normally comprised of a much larger number of relatively autonomous elements, which are highly interconnected and interact with each other (an organisation, industry, nation – there are plenty of examples). The systems are adaptive because the behaviour of the individual interacting agents changes in response to different events and what happens during the course of their interactions. They are also non-linear because the same action or condition can have varying effects upon outcomes. Peter Allen, a well-known UK complexity scholar, has offered a definition of a complex adaptive system, which has been frequently cited:

> What is a complex system? The answer is simple. It is any system that has within itself a capacity to respond to its environment in more than one way. This essentially means that it is not a mechanical system, with a single trajectory, but has some internal possibilities of choice or response that it can bring into play.

> (2001, p. 150)

Activity 2.5: Complex adaptive systems

Allow **5 minutes** for this activity.

Purpose: to consolidate your understanding of the definition of complex adaptive systems

Write down one or two examples of complex adaptive systems, and then compare your examples with those in the Discussion which follows.

Discussion

You may have cited others, but examples of complex adaptive systems can be found in nature and society. They include weather, ecological, biological, social, economic, industry and organisational systems. As medical researchers are only too aware, complex adaptive systems are everywhere in the micro-biological world ranging from relatively simple single organisms like viruses, to entire populations of bacteria. Such systems adapt to changes like a new vaccine by mutating. In the social and economic domain, these systems are comprised of interacting human beings. Examples include the economy, nations, cities, families and, of course, organisations.

Conventional and complexity perspectives on change

Having clarified what we mean by complexity by emphasising the adaptive nature of complex systems, we will now see how the complexity perspective explains how such adaptation, or change, takes place. It might be argued that organisational strategy is largely about making sense of change (for example, in the external environment) and managing change as the organisation moves forward into the future. As it does so, managers need to steer it in desirable directions (normally profitable ones) and avoid undesirable directions (those which would incur losses or threaten future survival and prosperity). This navigation exercise is conducted in uncertain and turbulent conditions. One of the major differences between complexity and other approaches to strategy is the way it understands this key issue of change in environments and organisations.

The conventional understanding of change

The conventional view of organisations and environments is that they approach change in a manner which resembles the journey of a frog. The frog may have an objective to cross a river. It takes a number of leaps forward as it moves from stone to stone, resting each time before it takes the next leap. In conventional thinking, organisations change by moving between equilibrium points in a manner analogous to the frog leaping from stone to stone.

This way of thinking envisages change as a process in which things like economic and industry environments move between equilibrium points through time in response to shocks caused by factors such as technological change, politics, changes in consumer preferences and so on.

As you will remember from Block 5, this image is captured by the 'theory of punctuated equilibrium', a term used to paint a picture of organisations in a more or less equilibrium state, undergoing incremental change for prolonged periods of time (Romanelli and Tushman, 1994). Periodically, this relative stability ('equilibrium') is punctuated by episodes of radical change after the processes of incremental strategy formulation lead an organisation to a point whereby it is out of tune with its environment – the phenomenon of 'strategic drift'. This usually results in some kind of crisis, forcing managers to recognise how out of step the organisation has become, and prompting strategic changes of a more radical nature to re-establish a good environmental fit.

This is often illustrated by a diagram (Figure 2.1), which charts change on the vertical axis and time on the horizontal one. An ascending diagonal line running from left to right from the joining of the axes represents environmental change. Another line looking like uneven steps, each of different height, represents the effect of incremental strategy development over a period of time. The diagram shows that realised strategy drifts out of alignment with the environment, at which point radical change is perceived to be needed.

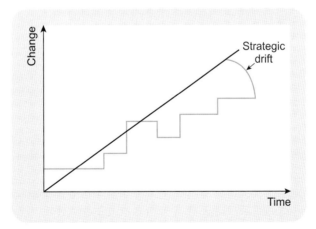

Figure 2.1: Strategic drift

The complexity understanding of change

The complexity understanding of how organisations change is different. Complexity views environments and organisations as dynamic complex adaptive systems, which are constantly changing in both incremental and radical ways. They are dynamic because they are interconnected and constantly evolving together rather than in isolation. They are not conceptualised in equilibrium terms. Unlike our image of the river-crossing frog, they never stand still – and neither do the stones (which might be wobbling under the frog's weight, or washed away by the river), the river (full of different currents) or the river banks (subject to erosion and potential collapse at any moment)!

Complex systems have many interacting elements, agents and sub-groups. Complexity analysis focuses upon their interactions and the interdependencies between them. In an organisation, the interacting 'agents' are individuals and decision-making sub-groups, which take decisions and actions in response to the specific problems and situations they face. As Waldrop points out, each agent in a complex adaptive system finds itself:

> … in an environment produced by its own interactions with other agents in the system. [Agents are] constantly acting and reacting to what other agents are doing.

> (1994, p. 145)

The image is different from logical incrementalism (Quinn, 1980) because it does not embody a notion of an actor taking logical small steps to get from A to some preconceived point B. Instead, the image is of actors and their environments evolving in tandem to some ultimately unknown point. The complexity metaphor for change is not punctuated equilibrium but evolution, or more precisely co-evolution. Just as the actions of a bee collecting nectar impact more widely upon the ecosystem in which it is nested (bees pollinate plants), so the actions of human agents and organisations impact upon the environments in which they are nested, even if they are unaware of what those impacts will be. This means that interactions between agents at the micro-level of the firm can lead to the emergence of new patterns of behaviour both within the firm and at the macro-levels of the industry environment or the economy. Similarly, interactions between agents in the wider industry and economic environment can lead to the emergence of new patterns of behaviour in those environments and within firms. The complexity conception of change is therefore co-evolutionary. No element in the system evolves in isolation from the others.

The dynamics driving change in complex systems are not the simple cause-and-effect dynamics of classical science. Instead they centre on the concept of feedback. Feedback is, of course, an important part of the conventional rational approach to strategy. It works to help organisations get their strategy back on track if it seems to be deviating from plan. So, for example, if halfway through the year it looks as if an expenditure budget is likely to be exceeded, then managers will take action to control costs. This is called negative feedback, and acts to dampen down activity (rather like a thermostat turning off a heating system once the required temperature has been exceeded). There is also positive feedback (though this is less common in conventional models of control) that acts to encourage and amplify activity – for example, praise and recognition for achievement in an appraisal interview is meant to consolidate and encourage good performance in an employee.

In complex adaptive systems, feedback (and particularly positive feedback) can develop its own momentum, rapidly multiplying its effects and escalating rapid development and transformation in ways which leave conventional understandings of change behind. An example from the natural sciences would be a chemical reaction. As the reaction gets underway, it generates heat which speeds up the reaction, which generates more heat, and so on. Positive feedback left unchecked in a system can rapidly create chaos – or, in the case of our chemical reaction example, an explosion.

A further point to bear in mind about feedback in complex adaptive systems is that its effect is often lagged. In other words, changes do not happen instantaneously – they may occur much later than the point at which feedback becomes available to the system. This further multiplies complexity and unpredictability in systems.

To sum up, complexity offers an understanding of environments and organisations as systems which adapt to change together. Organisations change to cope with environmental change, but the environment itself is changing as they do so. Furthermore, positive and negative feedback ensure that these changes influence both organisations and their environments in ways that are difficult to predict because of their potential subtlety and the timescales that may be involved. This is, to be sure, a lot more complicated than some other ways of envisaging the nature of change. But what use is it to managers? We now turn to the work of Richard Pascale, one of the most influential and widely-read writers on complexity, in order to answer this question.

Exploring the bedrock principles of complexity

US management scholar Richard Pascale sets out some practical consequences of complex adaptive systems in the article that forms Reading 18. We will widen our understanding of the concept by reading part of the article in Activity 2.6. Before we do so, it is worth taking note of the following information, which Pascale assumes his readers to know, but (depending on one's background and previous studies) may not be completely clear to all.

Early in the article, Pascale refers to Alfred Marshall's theory of industrial organisation as a strong influence on strategic thinking today. Marshall (1842–1924) was a pioneering UK economist whose ideas anticipated (among other things) Michael Porter's work on international comparative advantage (which you will remember from Block 2 Unit 3). Pascale challenges the economics-driven ideas of the positioning and resource-based views of strategy, arguing that their assumption of 'equilibrium' as the normal state of affairs is becoming irrelevant to contemporary business.

Another point that Pascale takes as read is familiarity with the term 'cybernetics'. This is, basically, the study of control mechanisms – things such as thermostats which regulate behaviour in systems. The word derives from the Ancient Greek word for 'helmsman'. As we have seen in our discussion, the idea of how a system is steered by feedback is an important element of complexity theory.

Activity 2.6: Four bedrock principles of complex adaptive systems

Allow **60 minutes** for this activity.

Purpose: to introduce the basic ideas on which Pascale builds his application of complexity theory to strategy

Read Reading 18, 'Surfing the edge of chaos' by Richard Pascale, up to, but not including, the paragraph headed 'Stable equilibrium equals death', and make notes in answer to the following points:

- What does Pascale list as the four properties of a complex adaptive system?

- List and explain the four 'bedrock principles relevant to new strategic work', which Pascale identifies.

Discussion

The four properties of a complex adaptive system (which all need to be present for it to count as such) are:

- They are comprised of many agents.

- They have multiple layers and levels.

- Unless replenished with energy, they are subject to entropy. In other words, if complex adaptive systems become too stable, they are vulnerable to extinction.

- They have the ability to recognise or sense patterns, enabling them to anticipate (but not predict) the future.

As Pascale points out, some systems are complex but not adaptive. To count as complex and adaptive a system must be able to anticipate and learn (like a mutating strain of bacteria becoming resistant to antibiotics).

The four bedrock principles (which Pascale spends the rest of his article illustrating with an extended example from the multinational oil company Shell) are as follows:

1 Equilibrium is a precursor to death for complex adaptive systems. For example, once an organisation becomes too stable it risks disaster by getting out of step with its changing environment.

2 Complex adaptive systems have the capacity to organise themselves, and generate more complexity. Think of a flock of starlings rising, swarming in the evening sky in complicated but coherent formations,

before settling again. Similarly, autonomous members of an organisation can behave in patterned ways from which interesting results can emerge.

3   Complex adaptive systems tend to move towards the edge of chaos. We will discuss what this implies more fully later in our treatment of complexity, but it is important to recognise that complexity has boundaries (what Pascale calls 'bounded instability'). In order to innovate, for example, organisations need to have enough, but not too much, instability – and they need to avoid the stagnation of equilibrium.

4   Finally, in Pascale's phrase, you 'can't direct a living system, only disturb it'. In other words, we need to accept that our effective control over an organisation, industry, or any other complex adaptive system, is limited. Instead of the Newtonian chains of cause and effect on which traditional strategy ideas are based, complexity holds the view that cause and effect is actually a lot less direct and predictable than we like to think. So, apparently trivial things can have strategic effects (as argued by strategy-as-practice scholars), and what might appear to be important things can have little or no effect, simply because of the complexity of the systems in which they occur.

It is necessary to unpack Pascale's 'bedrock principles' in order to explain why they imply such a radically different understanding of change from conventional theory as well as a different way to manage it. First, let's remind ourselves of what they are.

Activity 2.7: Consolidating bedrock principles

Allow **5 minutes** for this activity.

Purpose: to begin consolidating your understanding of Pascale's 'bedrock principles'

Without referring back to Activity 2.6 or Reading 18 for the time being, list below the four 'bedrock principles' enumerated by Pascale.

Then check back to confirm or correct your understanding.

Discussion

There is no feedback to this activity other than your own checking of your list.

Having refreshed our memory of the four bedrock principles, let us now put a bit more substance around the framework they represent.

Stable equilibrium equals death

Pascale notes that 'bounded instability' is more conducive to evolution than either stable equilibrium or 'explosive instability'. When organisations are too stable they lose their ability to be responsive and adapt. Remember that one of the characteristics of complex adaptive systems is that they are subject to entropy (i.e. loss of energy and ultimate decline). Without the injection of new energy of some kind (for example, a programme of strategic change to increase their competitiveness) they slow down and die. An example of this is Woolworths in the UK. The F. W. Woolworth Company was a retail chain founded in 1879. It was unable to adapt to increased competition during the 1980s and started to go into decline. In the UK, Woolworths survived until January 2009, but from the consumer perspective, it had not changed outwardly for many years. In terms of a complexity analysis, it was too stable and did not adapt to changed consumer demands. On the other hand, explosive instability leads to chaos, as illustrated by the global financial crisis of 2008. Here, as we will see in more detail in Box 2.2, the financial market's enthusiasm for the investment returns to be made from mortgage-backed securities led to instabilities, which rapidly spiralled out of control into catastrophic chaos.

Self-organisation and emergence

Complex adaptive systems are comprised of many agents creating lots of interactions at multiple levels. These multiple interactions follow simple rules, but are capable of generating complex emergent behaviour at the global level.

Consider geese flocking (see the following image). There are many individual interacting agents (in this case geese), each goose responding to the actions and movements of its neighbours. They interact with one another in accordance with very simple rules, providing 'bounded instability'. In a famous experiment, the US complexity researcher Craig Reynolds used a computer to simulate flocking behaviour by creature he called 'boids' and found that this could be achieved by individual agents following three simple steering rules in their interactions with each other (Reynolds, 1987). Birds 'self-organise' when they flock. There is no leader or central controller dictating where each bird should be or what it should do. The many individuals involved organise themselves with no central direction. Through the course of many interactions in accordance with simple rules at the local level of individual interactions, they produce a complex flocking behaviour at the global level. As a flock they are able to travel long distances, navigate around obstacles, adapt to wind currents and adverse weather conditions, and successfully migrate. Flocking is an example of emergence. In fact, it is an excellent example of an emergent strategy. Pascale (in Reading 18) documents how Shell facilitated 'self-organisation' at a local level in its retail operations to encourage emergent strategy.

The edge of chaos

Complex systems evolve to the edge of chaos. This is a concept that many people are aware of even if they have never previously taken an interest in complexity. It has been popularised in the mainstream management literature by Pascale and others, and has been considered in connection with innovation and change (e.g. McMillan and Carlisle, 2007; McMillan, 2008). This is one area in which complexity theory has been applied to the question: what does strategy need to achieve? To date, we have considered a number of ways in which complexity addresses limitations in conventional theories of strategic management. Our consideration of the edge of chaos concept offers an illustration of how management principles derived from complexity can also be radically different from those which emanate from the conventional rationality.

The edge of chaos is a systems state, on a continuum of possible states ranging from completely random to highly mechanistic and stable (see Figure 2.2). As a system moves towards chaos, its elements become ever more highly interconnected (McKelvey, 2001). The edge of chaos is a space in which new order emerges – so it is of particular interest to anyone studying essential strategic processes such as innovation and emergence.

At the mechanistic end of the continuum, a system is highly stable, ordered and resistant to change. At the random end of the continuum, there is apparent order at all. Using fractal geometry, a relati mathematics concerned with shapes and patterns (Ma mathematicians have been able to detect patterns in s events in chaotic systems (those operating in the chac As Box 2.1 suggests, truly random systems do not exi organisations – in spite of their unpredictability. In hui systems that are of interest are those depicted in the centre of Figure 2.2, namely hierarchical, complex and chaotic.

	Instability	Chaos	Edge of chaos	Edge of stability	Stability
Type of system	**Random**	**Chaotic**	**Complex**	**Hierarchical**	**Mechanistic**
Controlling mechanisms	None	Hard to detect	Largely self-organisation	Command and control	Tight rigid controls
Nature of relationships between agents	Independent agents; no detectable relationships	Volatile to random	Networked and highly connected	Formally dictated by top-down directives	Fixed and prescribed
Nature of interactions	Random and irregular	Some detectable regularities	Fluid and interdependent	Mostly dependent	Fully dependent
Outcome	Random changes and outcomes; disintegration likely	Instability – unstable changes and outcomes	Flexible new order involving radical and/or incremental changes	Stability – incremental changes	Stability – mechanistic systems are resistant to change; ossification likely

Figure 2.2: Types of system and degrees of order and stability (Source: adapted from McMillan and Carlisle, 2007)

Take a moment to study Figure 2.2 from the point of view of your own experience of human organisations as systems (relating it to your workplace, family or any other organisation of which you are a member or have experience). Where would you place your chosen organisation on the continuum and why? Many of today's organisations are trying to get away from being overly hierarchical to move into a more flexible 'complex' position, in order to be more effective in the dynamic environment of the twenty-first century. Their ability to do this may differ. For some (e.g. the armed services or police force), command and control as a management mechanism makes sense; as do formal relationships between members. For others (such as advertising agencies or arts organisations), the need for creativity encourages a more 'chaotic' structure. However, even in such organisations managers exert tight discipline to ensure that deadlines are met and budgets honoured. Similarly, in contemporary family life many parents seek to establish more open, democratic relationships with their children than might have been the case in previous generations. In spite of the move away from strict hierarchy, however, there is still a need for respect and boundaries. When families stop operating as they should, social workers often refer to the result as 'chaotic'.

Most human systems, such as organisations and economies, are normally complex rather than chaotic in our highly interconnected and networked world. As we have noted, complex systems tend to evolve to the edge of chaos on the continuum shown in Figure 2.2. In this state, they are highly adaptive. However, the risk is that they can tip over the edge of chaos into actual chaos for a time. A chaotic system is one in which wholly unpredictable behaviour has arisen. Complex systems can and do periodically tip into chaos. The key to keeping a complex system like an organisation productively sub-chaotic is to maintain an appropriate tension between flexibility and control, whereas traditional strategic thinking emphasises control only (usually through negative feedback).

Box 2.1: Patterns in chaos

Our ability to detect at least some regularities (patterns) in chaotic systems is important. As Pascale points out, pattern recognition enables complex systems to anticipate and prepare for unpredictable events. For example, when the precise 'causes' for each occurrence of a stock market crash are analysed with the benefit of hindsight, they are often found to be uniquely different in each case. Nonetheless, stock markets crash from time to time (this is a pattern). They do so unpredictably and the precipitating 'causes' are invariably never the same each and every time a crash occurs. Bull runs and bear runs are a pattern. A bull market is a market characterised by rising prices, which encourages speculators to buy now in the hope of selling later at a profit. A bear market is one with falling prices, encouraging sales now to forestall future losses. When bull runs end, stock markets can crash (this is also a pattern). Bull runs do not 'cause' stock markets to crash in the Newtonian sense. Furthermore, markets don't necessarily crash every time a bull run occurs. However, after a bull run ends, they may. Volatility is built into the very nature of markets and economies. We cannot predict them, but we can qualitatively recognise patterns.

Weak links of cause and effect

Complexity science suggests that we are not, and possibly never will be, in control of the world around us. Small, almost imperceptible, events occurring in a complex system operating at the edge of chaos can have unpredictable effects, which can push them over the edge. The classic visualisation of the 'butterfly effect', whereby a butterfly flapping its wings in Brazil sets off a tornado in Texas (Lorenz, 1963), provides a metaphor for a very small disturbance having massive effects elsewhere in a system. This sums up the way that complex systems are adaptive. Self-organising agents produce novel emergent structures and behaviours. Both incremental and radical change can take place, but their behaviour is not random. Complexity is a state of 'bounded instability', to cite Pascale. In the world of human affairs, this is the state in which those systems which can adapt to change operate most of the time. In the very short term, some degree of prediction is possible. However, complex systems can lapse into actual chaos. In this state, their behaviour is wildly unpredictable even in the short term. The implication for this as far as strategy is concerned is to recast managers as facilitators of emergent strategy rather than designers and directors of deliberate strategy.

Now let's try to recognise complexity at work in a brief case study of the crisis that overtook global financial markets in 2008 (Box 2.2).

Box 2.2: A brief complexity analysis of the financial crisis

The global financial crisis of 2008 provides an example of how a living system in the world of human affairs moved to the edge of chaos when presented with an opportunity. It then tipped over the edge into actual chaos in response to a small system disturbance. Prior to the sub-prime mortgage crisis, which emerged in the USA in 2006, US mortgage lenders were presented with big opportunities to boost profits by responding to environmental changes. For example, foreign money had flowed into the West from Asia. Money supply was high while interest rates were kept low. Deregulation had allowed the banks to accept higher risk borrowers and take advantage of 'securitisation' (an investment-product innovation which enabled securities market investors to benefit from the housing boom). However, securitisation also complicated the mortgage-lending process. It introduced many more levels and layers of interaction and created many more interdependencies than had existed in the traditional lender-borrower era. Complex systems become ever more highly interconnected and develop greater numbers of interdependencies as they move towards the edge of chaos. The advent of securitisation moved the complex system of mortgage lending towards chaos – and beyond.

Securitisation turned a mortgage, which provides an income stream but also carries a default liability, into a product which could be sold to investors for a premium over and above the loan amount. 'Mortgage-backed securities' were sold to investors in global securities markets. However, because traditional retail banking (savings and loans) and investment banking were no longer conducted by separate institutions in many cases, the separation of income streams from liabilities became illusory.

Some banks began aggressively selling mortgages to borrowers who had little hope of meeting long-term repayments. The banks selling the mortgages would profit by selling them on through the securitisation process. Because property prices were rising, it was assumed that borrowers unable to repay their loans would, in a rising property market, be able to sell their properties. If they defaulted and their properties were repossessed, it was assumed that the debts outstanding could easily be recouped. Although securitisation began with packaging mortgage debt and income streams as an investment product ('mortgage-backed securities'), the product itself became more complicated as other forms of debt were added to investment packages. These new investment products became more complicated, opaque and difficult to evaluate.

In terms of complexity thinking, this was short-sighted. A small disturbance in the system always had the potential to destabilise it. Complexity thinking might have alerted the financial world to the systemic risk. However, conventional (Newtonian-inspired) economic modelling had convinced the financial world that an asset price collapse in the property market was a 'non-probable' event and that default rates would remain low. The sub-prime mortgage crisis occurred because lending was founded upon the assumption that existing trends would continue along predicted trajectories. Property prices would continue to rise. Default rates would remain more or less within a forecast range. The conventional models acknowledged the fact that alternative scenarios were possible, but assessed the probability of them occurring to be so small as to be an insignificant consideration in strategic decision making. Complexity thinking considers patterns. Although one cannot predict precisely when events will occur, asset prices do periodically collapse as well as rise. Periods of extreme exuberance in asset markets are sometimes, albeit not always, followed by periods of gloom and asset price collapse. Interest rates rise and fall.

It is now a matter of history that a small systems disturbance occurred in the form of an interest rate rise in the USA. This led to an increase in the mortgage default rate among sub-prime borrowers and, concurrently, a rise in default rates for other types of debt which had been packaged as investment products alongside mortgage-backed securities. Because securitised investment products had been bought by investors in securities markets worldwide, the rising default rates would have repercussions worldwide. This small disturbance cascaded through the financial system in a 'butterfly effect'. From the chaos that ensued, a new order began to emerge with mergers and takeovers and government financial bail-outs. The financial collapse of 2008 is an example of complexity in action.

(Source: adapted and expanded from Carlisle, 2010)

Insights on strategy from complexity theory

All four principles of complex adaptive systems (equilibrium as death, self-organisation, the tendency to move towards chaos, and unpredictability) have implications for our understanding of strategy and how it should be managed. Had the financial managers in Box 2.2 been more conversant with such principles they might have behaved more circumspectly and avoided a catastrophe.

Our discussion of the four principles in this section has underlined the importance of:

- resisting too much stability (for example, from too rigid a culture)

- working with, rather than against, emerging strategy

- balancing flexibility with order

- accepting that there are limits to what we can hope to control.

Each of these implications, depending on your point of view, either challenges or complements more traditional notions of strategy.

An example of how complexity theory complements existing notions of strategy is the way it explains something which the Resource-Based View (RBV) of strategy claims but does not explain. You will remember how the RBV argues that strategies at firm-level can shape the environment of the firm. The RBV does not quite explain how this happens. The complexity paradigm offers the dynamic of co-evolution to explain how firms can influence environments and to explain how minor disturbances at firm-level can have large global-level impacts on the environment of the industry or economy. It therefore adds to conventional understanding. Complexity explains the emergence of new behaviours and structures, which were never planned (with both desirable and undesirable consequences). The rest of this section develops the topic of how complexity sheds new light on strategy – how it is formed, what the key strategic capabilities are for an organisation, and how organisations can manage innovation.

A complexity perspective on strategy formation

As we have seen throughout this module, the focus of strategy process research is on trying to find out how strategy takes place. The thinking behind such research is that if we knew more about how strategy develops in successful organisations, we might be able to abstract some principles and apply them more widely (accepting, of course, that there might be limits to the generalisability of such rules). A constant theme in this research is the balance between deliberate and emergent strategy. In particular, the concept of emergent strategy strikes many as a realistic picture of practice, but not very useful as a guide to managing strategy. One of the great hopes attached to complexity theory as a way of understanding strategy is the light it sheds on emergence, and the principles managers can take from this in order to manage emergent strategy more effectively.

The conventional approach to strategy sees it as beginning with some kind of mission or set of goals, followed by deliberate stages of analysis, choice and implementation, a framework with which you will be familiar from the structure of this module, and which is illustrated in Figure 2.3. When applied in organisations, complexity thinking makes different assumptions about the requirements for the formulation of effective strategy. This is because it focuses upon strategy's emergence not its deliberate formulation. It emphasises the importance of facilitating the development of strategy. This can happen by promoting effective learning processes, which lead to the questioning of assumptions, or by fostering the adaptive co-evolutionary complexity dynamics of self-organisation and emergence.

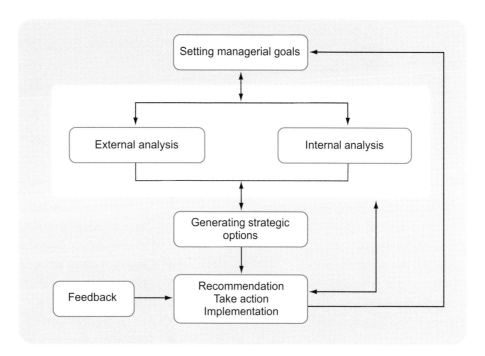

Figure 2.3: An iterative process model

The classical approach to strategy assumes that strategy either is or should be largely deliberate or planned. It recognises that emergent strategy does arise, but its tools and techniques are not designed to foster emergent strategy from the bottom of the organisational pyramid. They have tended to be offered as tools for senior managers to use in the formulation of planned rational strategies. When managers adopt a complexity approach to the development of strategy, fostering emergent strategy from the bottom up is a key objective.

Many of the approaches to emergent strategy development that have been proposed in the complexity literature afford a central place to sense-making and learning. One of the reasons for this is because emergent strategy can lead just as easily to undesirable outcomes as to desirable ones, unless effective sense-making and learning take place. Because of this, some complexity models of strategy development focus more upon the processes of learning and sense-making than upon analysis and evaluation.

Downs et al. (2003) outline an approach to helping desirable emergent strategy develop. As we will see in Activity 2.8, they use the terms 'symbols' and 'symbol systems' in the list of stages that makes up their model of how strategy takes place. These terms are connected to the kind of sense-making processes we discussed in Block 1 – and also to the way in which different organisational cultures give symbolic meanings to aspects of organisational life, from car parking spaces to weekly sales figures. What Downs et al. are stressing in this choice of words is that there is more to the information input to the strategising process than the objective facts and figures assumed by the rational model. Managers interpret, and choose, a kind of 'symbolic' reality according to their view of the world – they are not detached from the world as the rational model assumes.

Activity 2.8: Managing emergent strategy development

Allow 10 minutes for this activity.

Purpose: to compare complexity and conventional approaches to strategy development in order to better understand how to manage emergent strategy

Briefly note the differences and similarities between the two models below:

A complexity approach

1 Sense a possible threat or opportunity
2 Choose a symbol system
3 Decide on a model
4 Draw out the symbols
5 Reflect on the symbols
6 Interpret the message
7 Decide on an action
8 Act
9 Repeat cycle after acting

A conventional approach

1 Set managerial goals
2 Conduct internal analysis
3 Conduct external analysis
4 Generate strategic options
5 Decide on course of action
6 Implement action
7 Collect feedback
8 Repeat process in light of feedback

(Source: adapted from Downs et al., 2003)

Discussion

In some respects the two models are remarkably similar. They both describe iterative processes. They both outline steps or stages that are sequential. The conventional model focuses upon objective analysis and choice. The complexity model focuses upon sense-making and learning in the development of emergent strategy. Mintzberg, in 'Crafting strategy' (Reading 5) considers emergent strategy to be essentially unplanned and unintended. He defines it as emerging from a pattern of actions. Downs et al. (2003) indicate that strategy can also emerge from the ways in which organisational members interpret meaningful events. Complexity approaches to emergent strategy development typically focus upon managing the contexts in which learning occurs. Downs et al. (2003) highlight the fact that double-loop learning (or 'complex' learning as we might call it) often requires us to question assumptions that we would normally take for granted. The important point to take away from this is that unquestioned assumptions underpin much of what we do. We often make sense of situations in the light of such assumptions without even realising it. The importance of sense-making in the strategy process has already been highlighted in Block 1. The development of effective emergent strategy often requires an ability on the part of organisational members to question existing assumptions, not only about how things should be done in the organisation, but also about the place of conventional thinking in how they make sense of the world. It is a clear, practical invitation to the kind of critical thinking whose value we have stressed throughout the module.

A complexity perspective on strategic capabilities

Complexity approaches focus upon building an organisation in which diversity is fostered, effective learning takes place and self-organisation is encouraged as a method of problem solving. Conventional approaches tend to focus upon simplifying problems and using reductionist thinking, and objective models, methods, tools and techniques to arrive at an acceptable solution. Complexity approaches focus upon recognising emergence and allowing it to blossom so that it can be built upon. Conventional approaches focus upon a rational analysis of different parts of the organisation which will deliver a planned strategy. Complexity approaches try to keep bureaucratic rules and procedures to a minimum to give individuals maximum discretion and minimum constraint in building upon successful emergence. Conventional management can snuff out emergence, in an effort to ensure that rationally planned strategies are delivered. In short, conventional management is primarily concerned with control; complexity-inspired management with emergence. Table 2.1 summarises these differences in what either approach sees as the required capabilities of an organisation. Unsurprisingly, conventional management and complexity management are sometimes held as alternatives in the literature.

Table 2.1: Comparing conventional and complexity approaches to strategy

	Conventional approach	Complexity approach
Management inspiration	Rational scientific paradigm	Quantum physics, chaos and complexity sciences
Tacit assumptions	The world is essentially linear and hierarchical and can be adequately understood in terms of cause and effect	The world is one of complex non-linear relationships Agents and elements are highly interconnected and interdependent We need a holistic or whole systems appreciation and understanding
Approach to problem solving	Simplify Use reductionist thinking, and objective methods, models, tools and techniques	Accept complexity and subjectivity Foster diversity, self-organisation and co-evolutionary emergence
Aims in problem solving	Find procedures and solutions to implement based upon a rational analysis of different parts of the organisation	Find creative approaches based upon a holistic appreciation of the organisation in its environment and their interconnectedness
Key management role	Manage change by rational planning and the exercise of control	Manage co-evolutionary adaptation and emergence by giving individuals maximum discretion and exercising minimum constraint in accordance with simple rules

(Source: adapted from Carlisle, 2010)

Activity 2.9: Complex vs conventional approaches to strategy

Allow **5 minutes** for this activity.

Purpose: to consider whether conventional and complexity approaches are radical alternatives

Spend two or three minutes forming an opinion on the following question: Are the conventional and complexity approaches to strategy development really alternatives?

Discussion

You might feel that they are alternatives because the thinking which underpins them is so different. They make different assumptions about the nature of the world and human beings, and the ways in which they interact within organisations.

On the other hand, in practice, organisations do develop both intended and unintended strategy. Some strategies are planned. Others emerge. Within the conventional strategy paradigm, the development of effective emergent strategy has been a relatively neglected area. Therefore, you might conclude that complexity can address this neglect, and in this sense be complementary. Furthermore, the systems approach which complexity offers can provide explanations for things which are part of the unexplained 'black box' in other better established strategic theories (a 'black box' in this sense represents those things which go on in a process but remain largely unexplained). An example of such a black box which we mentioned at the end of the last section is the unexplained claim by RBV theorists that organisations shape their environments. Complexity theory explains this by pointing out how self-organising interacting agents during the course of many interactions can produce emergent behaviours and structures at the global level. The main focus for research in complexity science is the dynamics of interactions between elements of complex adaptive systems; the 'Boid' simulation example mentioned earlier is one of the best known (Reynolds, 1987).

A complexity perspective on innovation

Stacey (2007) describes how structure emerges from apparent chaos through positive and negative feedback. Out of chaos, a new order emerges. Thus a certain amount of chaos in the business environment can be productive in terms of innovation. If we follow this prescription, the task of strategic managers seeking productive innovation is to keep the organisation operating at the 'edge of chaos' without it tipping over the edge into actual chaos.

At the edge of chaos, there is sufficient cohesion to keep the organisation operating in a broad general strategic direction, with the inclusion of enough chaos or variation to foster innovation. Indeed, Pascale et al. (2001) argue that innovation is born at the nexus of stability and chaos.

The same authors recommend that managers should foster effective innovation through complex adaptive processes like self-organisation, advocating looser structures in turbulent environments. Managers unfamiliar with complexity thinking sometimes have problems with this suggestion as they can see it as 'relinquishing control'. The traditional concept of control is, as we noted earlier, associated with negative feedback. In some areas of a business this is entirely appropriate. In the private sector, businesses need to make a profit. Costs need to be controlled. However, in other areas attempts to exercise tight control over activities can be counterproductive because they stifle adaptive innovation.

There is an important distinction to be made between tight control and coordination. A simple way of stating this point is that complexity thinking suggests that effective managers allow the maximum degree of freedom or autonomy possible in any given situation. They seek to coordinate activities without compromising those essential bottom-line areas (e.g. budgets) in which it is necessary to exercise control.

In terms of complexity thinking this is important because control is a stabilising influence, which pushes the system towards the mechanistic end of the spectrum shown in Figure 2.2 above. In turbulent environments, organisations that are too stable stagnate, unable to adapt to the changes around them. This complexity implication runs counter to what often happens in turbulent times. Frequently, managers in organisations experiencing turbulence in their environments become more bureaucratic and controlling. Complexity suggests that in doing so they can stifle the development of those behaviours which could enable the organisation to prosper and thrive.

Activity 2.10: Applying complexity thinking

Allow **60 minutes** for this activity.

Purpose: to complete your reading and note taking for Reading 18

Now turn back to Reading 18, Pascale's 'Surfing the Edge of Chaos', and resume your reading from the paragraph headed 'Stable equilibrium equals death' to the end of the article.

As you read, make notes on how well you feel the example of Steve Miller's work at Shell exemplifies the bedrock principles, which we have been discussing.

Discussion

You will no doubt form your own view of the effectiveness of Pascale's running illustration of his bedrock principles, depending on how convinced you are by complexity theory as an idea, but here are some reflections you may find useful:

In 1996, Miller found Shell at the end of a two-year attempted transformation programme that had not worked. The 'business as usual' attitude and impenetrable culture were both warnings of complacency, in spite of the intense competition the downstream business faced. The country-by-country structure allowed country heads to prevent change from above. These are good examples of an organisation facing dangerous equilibrium – though it's difficult not to believe that different aspects of the business might show more or less dynamism (for example, some of the country heads might have had relatively successful strategies in place).

Miller's decision to get directly involved with customer-facing managers around the group, to shift the focus of activity to the front lines, sounds like a practical way of tapping the capacity of self-organisation, and Pascale mentions that the first wave of initiatives spawned others (a good example of self-organisation leading to emerging complexity). It has to be said, however, that his 'fishbowl' approach acted as a filter to select some ideas and adjust others in ways which might have reflected senior management thinking at the expense of the periphery. On the other hand, if (as complexity theory suggests) managers need to keep a productive tension between control and flexibility to promote innovation, perhaps this is what it looks like in practice.

Pascale's illustration of how Shell's downstream operation moved to the edge of chaos revisits the fishbowl process – underlining the stress it created on all concerned. This acknowledgement of the emotional dimension of the edge of chaos is worth noting. It seems to have galvanised the organisation given the support of senior management, but it sounds like a high-risk strategy which would be difficult to maintain for any length of time. How do you think it would play in an organisation you have experience of?

Finally, the difficulty of controlling a complex adaptive system, because of the weak ties between cause and effect, seems (at least to me) less convincingly illustrated – perhaps because it is almost paradoxical to expect to exert any control at all. Miller admits that up to 60 per cent of his time is spent on initiatives that offer no guarantee of results. If I were a shareholder, I would find that worrying. On the other hand, he also likens himself to the helmsman of a ship (in an attempt to express the scale of the operation), which suggests that he does imagine himself in control (even though he claims this is a different kind of control from traditional leadership). What do you think?

Feedback to Activity 2.1

If you have completed Activity 2.1, you will have written what amounts to a summary of our account of complexity in this material. You might like to compare your response to the activity with the feedback below and check if there is anything missing.

- Complexity thinking focuses upon interconnectedness between systems elements rather than simple cause and effect.

- Complexity's perspective on change emphasises interdependence.

- Complexity is concerned with properties that make systems adaptive.

- Complexity deals with non-linear relationships.

- Complexity dynamics are different from classical cause-and-effect dynamics. They include self-organisation, emergence and co-evolution. These properties mean that complex systems cannot be directed, merely disturbed.

- Complexity explains how and why small disturbances can have major unpredicted effects.

- Conventional thinking applied to management focuses primarily upon planning and control. Complexity thinking focuses upon emergent strategy, how to foster and develop it, and how to recognise and build on desirable emergence. This has been relatively neglected in conventional management.

- Complexity theorists are concerned with multiple interdependencies, multiple interactions, multiple cause-and-effect relationships, and multiple feedback loops.

- Complex adaptive processes (like self-organisation) can lead to effective emergent behaviours and structures – for example, explaining how organisations can change their environments as claimed by the RBV of strategy.

- Complexity theory results in new normative recommendations for managerial action (for example, facilitation rather than direction).

Complexity thinking implies a different approach to strategy, management and the management of change from that which is implied by the conventional rational approach.

In Activity 2.8, our comparison of the conventional approach to strategy development with a complexity learning approach highlighted the need for organisational learning and the questioning of assumptions in sense-making (a crucial process in strategy) . One of the key challenges is in developing appropriate 'simple rules' to provide the 'bounded instability' mentioned by Pascale in Reading 18.

Although complexity science began to emerge as a serious force in the natural sciences during the 1960s, its application to management problems is much more recent. It is as yet an underdeveloped perspective in management studies. The hope of those who work in the area must be that complexity might eventually address the limitations of conventional management thinking in a manner analogous to the way in which it has addressed the limitations of classical science in physics and the natural sciences.

2.2: Strategy as discourse

Complexity theory is one direction in which some contemporary strategy theorists are discovering new insights to add to our understanding of strategic processes and effective ways of promoting them. In this section, we are going to explore another direction, which is also engaging a considerable amount of interest in the academic strategy as practice community. If complexity theory takes its inspiration from the natural sciences to theorise organisations and their environments as complex adaptive systems, strategy as practice takes its inspiration from the social sciences – to explain what goes on in strategy as human, social activity. In this section, we will focus in particular on how the very human activity of telling and following stories (narrative) shapes the performance of strategy, and thus how best we can manage it.

A practice-focused view of strategy

In Block 1, you were introduced to an emerging idea that is taking hold among certain strategy scholars, which is that one means of better understanding what strategists actually do is to see strategy work as comprising three key elements: practitioners, practices and praxis (Whittington, 2006). In Block 5, we examined practitioners in more depth, by looking at just who strategists are and what they do. In this section, we will delve further into what is meant by praxis, which in a strategy context is mainly concerned with the daily and sometimes mundane acts that strategists have to undertake to accomplish their strategy work. Praxis can be the brief conversations held between strategists, email exchanges, report writing or verbal feedback sessions commonly witnessed at workshops. Note how many of these activities involve writing or speaking – in other words, using language to accomplish things. The recent refocusing on what strategists actually do can be seen as part of a wider 'linguistic turn' evident in other areas of management and organisation scholarship where researchers have started to pay more attention to the role of language as an activity in itself.

The practice-focused definition of strategy put forward in Block 1 described it as a 'situated, socially accomplished activity' (Jarzabkowski et al., 2007, p. 11) and it is the socially accomplished aspect we will focus on in this section. The main argument advanced here is that in seeing strategy as something that is socially accomplished, the nature of that social accomplishment needs to be identified and understood. Scholars doing this are converging around the view that strategy is actually constituted and progressed through discourse among and between strategists, understood in the broadest possible terms, so it is this we will concentrate on. However, before we do this, a little bit of context-setting is called for, so in the section below we will consider the wider 'linguistic turn' in the social sciences and what this means for our understanding of what goes on inside our increasingly complex organisations. By working through this section, you will have developed a more rounded understanding of strategy, one that resonates with what Whittington (2001) calls the systemic theory of strategy.

The linguistic turn

What is becoming referred to as the 'linguistic turn' in management and organisation research has its roots in particular forms of philosophy and sociology. The influential twentieth-century philosopher Ludwig Wittgenstein is often seen as one of the early forerunners of the linguistic turn. Wittgenstein questioned and sought to identify the relationship between language and reality, a key theme that underpins the linguistic turn. It was an issue that he constantly returned to in developing his ideas. Wittgenstein argued that the problems philosophers deal with are not created by the nature of reality, but by the nature of language. Language, in this sense, creates reality; it does not represent reality.

This may seem like a rather controversial notion. How can language 'create' reality? Our common-sense understanding of language is that it is simply a way of communicating our perceptions and ideas to one another. This common-sense view of language sees it as a transparent medium for transmitting what is already there, rather than as something through which reality is created. Language represents reality – and we have dictionaries to prove it. But there is another way of looking at language, which emphasises its role as an activity. You can use language to do things – quite apart from conveying the literal meaning of the words used. Think of the number of different ways you could be greeted on arrival at work by someone using the same words: 'Good morning'. The phrase could be used to greet you warmly as a colleague, or formally to indicate distance between you and someone higher up the organisation's hierarchy, or by a stranger to open up a conversation, or even ironically to refer to the fact that you are rolling in late (possibly even in the afternoon). What we can do with language extends beyond giving different meanings to a common phrase, however. We have already mentioned in Block 1 how talking or writing about organisations that 'have' a strategy creates a different set of expectations for what strategy is, or should be, from that created by talking or writing about organisations that 'do' strategy. This is a good example of how language can be used to exclude some ways of understanding reality, and include others. This is what we mean when we say that language is constitutive of reality, not just representational of it. In fact, some theorists would go so far as to argue that because language is the only way we have to gain access to reality (through verbalising our perceptions, whether to ourselves in thought or to others) to all intents and purposes, language literally does create reality.

Like the scientific tradition from which it is descended, the classical, traditional approach to strategy takes a less sophisticated view of language. It takes it as read that language is merely representational, not constitutive. What this means is the assumption that the language used to convey strategy concepts and ideas has no influence on the concepts and ideas themselves. This is why many papers and books in the classical tradition are often an extremely 'dry' read, as the author strives for a detached, neutral writing style.

The linguistic turn in the social sciences argues that reality exists in the language(s) we use to construct it. From a linguistic perspective, as we draw on new and different vocabularies we create a new and different reality. Simply put, according to this perspective, we talk realities into being. Therefore, if we talk in a different way we create a different reality. Wittgenstein described language as a series of games, each with its own rules. Knowing the rules of the game is important if we are to join in with how an issue is discussed. I'm sure you will have had the experience of feeling excluded from a conversation from time to time because of the jargon being used – whether this is 'tecchie talk' or 'youth speak' or even 'management buzzwords'. These are ways in which participants play language games according to rules which exclude others while heightening and confirming their own realities. The 'rules of the game' is a theme we will return to later when we identify strategy as discourse, and consider how some discourses are assigned legitimacy and authority, while others are marginalised. In Wittgenstein's terms, what people who espouse the dominant discourse have done is establish their own rules of the game as the primary one within the organisation.

For those academics that advance the linguistic turn as their preferred ontological assumption (the way the world works), the idea of transferring classical science's epistemology (its theory of how knowledge is created within the world) poses problems. Let's illustrate this with an example. You may recall in Unit 1 of this block our discussion of forecasting included a brief description of how Schuster (1906), among others, identified a regular pattern in the magnitude of sunspots and was able to predict their continuation through time-series analysis. This success in the natural science field was felt by early researchers to be replicable in the social science arena. The same techniques of detached analysis that identified the sunspot sequences have been used to supposedly predict human behaviour. An ontological problem the proponents of this approach seem to ignore away is that social situations involving people doing things are inherently unpredictable (the way the social world works is different from the way the natural world works). Also, Schuster's observations didn't affect the pattern in the magnitude of the sunspots, this occurred whether he was watching it or not. In social situations, however, things are not quite so simple. The presence of a researcher does affect people's behaviour – the Hawthorne effect illustrates this (Landsberger, 1958), see Box 2.3. This makes the idea of predicting behaviour, which was possible for Schuster and colleagues studying the natural sciences, problematic for researchers in the social sciences, whose theory of how knowledge is created in the world (epistemology) holds that social researchers cannot stand apart from the phenomena they study.

Box 2.3: Illuminating behaviour at work

The Hawthorne experiments were a series of pioneering studies that took place between 1924 and 1932 funded by the Western Electric Company at its Chicago Hawthorne plant. The first experiment (1924–7) looked at the effect of different levels of lighting conditions on productivity. Some surprising results led the researchers to conclude that changing the level of lighting had less effect on productivity than the fact that the workers knew they were being observed – which made them very productive indeed. Thus was born the term 'The Hawthorne Effect', defined as the tendency for human subjects to change their behaviour simply as a consequence of the presence of researchers. This is one of the key things that differentiates social science research from research carried out into the natural sciences.

(Source: adapted from Landsberger, 1958)

Linguistic scholars are not interested in predicting behaviour, but analysing it to draw insights that may be useful for practitioners and academics in other contexts. Generalisability, the holy grail of science (i.e. seeking to establish hard and fast laws which hold in all circumstances), is simply not an issue for linguistic researchers. Their goal is to create plausible narratives that get close to describing how and why managers, for example, do what they do. Linguistic researchers should always qualify their research claims by stating that what they have produced is a partial account of what they have researched, not the account. They should always acknowledge that other researchers (or, indeed, themselves on another occasion) could very well produce a different research narrative, one that uses a different form of words (language) than what they have produced this time. By writing at all, linguistic researchers claim, we create fictions; this applies equally to researchers, managers and imaginative writers (again, we will return to this later).

The linguistic turn, then, offers an alternative social science approach to studying human organisations than that based on the natural sciences. Following Wittgenstein, it generates renewed interest in, and respect for, the significance of language, stories and narrative in how people make sense of their worlds and make their lives meaningful at home and work. The adherents of this approach claim that we make sense of our lives through telling each other stories. For example, if we move house to a new area, we learn about it, both before and after the move, through talking to people to hear their stories, reading about it on the internet or in local newspapers, and then discussing these stories with others. We integrate our personal experiences, motivations, hopes and desires, with what we have heard and read to create a coherent narrative in which we can locate ourselves. Through such acts we make our lives in a new house meaningful. Linguistic researchers claim we undertake the same storytelling activities focused on making our lives meaningful when we are in the workplace too. This research focus has led to the development of narrative theory or narratology (Fisher, 1987).

Walter Fisher, a US sociologist, has written widely about the topic of communication and is considered one of the founders of narratology. His work offers an alternative to the much-quoted idea that human behaviour is best understood through economic theories. These depict men and women as rational and broadly self-interested actors who have the ability to make judgements towards their subjectively defined ends. Fisher drew from the ideas of Alasdair MacIntyre (a philosopher famous for his criticism of modern trends) to challenge the idea that human behaviour is best understood in economic terms and offered an alternative based on a different underpinning concept.

MacIntyre asserted that men and women are essentially storytelling animals and Fisher (1984) developed this idea to create the label 'Homo narrans' (storytelling human being) as an alternative to the more commonly used 'Homo economicus'. For Fisher, and proponents of the role of language in organisations, this moves the focus from seeing humans as mere economic (re)actors to seeing them as complex narrative meaning-makers. The narrative view suggests that people accomplish their work in organisations through telling stories to each other. These are not necessarily stories in the traditional sense, though they may include these. They are stories in the sense that they use linguistic means to make sense of things and establish appropriate future actions.

Activity 2.11: One kind of strategic storytelling

Allow **15 minutes** for this activity.

Purpose: to illustrate storytelling of a traditional kind in an organisation

Please access the module website to view the media clip, 'The impact of strategic storytelling' from Professor Jay Conger (Conger, 2006).

There is a transcript of the clip on the website, should you need to refer to it.

As you watch the clip, make notes in answer to the following questions:

- What does Conger claim to be the advantages of storytelling over other forms of sharing information in an organisation?

- This is one way of telling one sort of a story in an organisation. What other kinds of stories do people tell, share and act out in organisational life?

Discussion

Conger recounts a very specific story, told by Herb Kelleher of Southwest Airlines, in order to explain pricing levels and position the organisation in the minds of customers and, perhaps more importantly, employees. It's a very literal version of storytelling, but it is one of the ways available to people in organisations to articulate and implement strategy. Its main advantage over statistics, PowerPoint presentations and documents is that it is memorable in a way they are not.

Conger's example is a story in the traditional sense, but other stories are being played out all the time in organisations – guiding how things are made sense of and appropriate future actions are decided upon. What about the story of your own career, or those of your co-workers or boss? What kinds of stories get told at meetings? Are you writing the story of your professional résumé by studying, for example, or undertaking specific sorts of work in order to get 'experience' to move on to something else? Or how about an organisation with which you are familiar as a worker or user? Is it engaged on a story of expansion, or is it trapped in a story of decline? What about its products or services? The famous 'product life cycle' model you may have come across, if you have ever studied marketing, maps out the life story of a product in a way designed to help choose the appropriate marketing activity to support each stage.

In organisational studies, the idea that people in firms progress their work through telling stories about what they do is a well-established research field. It has resulted in Currie and Brown (2003, p. 579) suggesting that organisations themselves can be usefully conceptualised as 'storytelling milieux'. By this they mean that one way to frame organisations and the people in them is to see them as sites where people are engaged in constant narrative interactions, literally where individuals and groups are unceasingly talking with one another, listening to each other, reading, writing and thinking in stories. The linguistic turn in management research, then, refers to those scholars who believe the most effective way of understanding what happens in organisations is to listen to and analyse the stories organisational actors tell when they are engaged in their normal daily activities. For them, it is the people inside organisations that create and renew them through their storytelling. So, to understand strategy, linguistic researchers would argue, we must understand the stories that are created about and around it.

While still a minority view among writers and thinkers on strategy, it is a perspective that is growing and likely to become more important in future years. Researchers who work within the linguistic turn are offering interesting insights, but these can be difficult to reconcile with more traditional conceptualisations of strategy. This is perhaps one of the ongoing challenges facing strategy academics: how to reconcile these differing views in a useful and meaningful way. From your perspective as a student, I would suggest that you need to be aware that the narrative view is one of the alternatives to the dominant economics-inspired version of strategy, and that through using it in your investigations you will be better able to understand what is happening in your own organisation, from which you can then take action.

Strategy as storytelling

In 1997, the leading US academic journal, the *Academy of Management Review,* published a paper that challenged the traditional view of strategy head on. The article's title, 'Strategy retold: toward a narrative view of strategic discourse', clearly sets out the authors' (David Barry and Michael Elmes) argument: that a framing of strategy from a narrative perspective retells strategy. They make a number of telling points that cause us to question our assumptions about what strategy may be.

They assert that 'strategy must rank as one of the most prominent, influential, and costly stories told in organisations' (Barry and Elmes, 1997, p. 430). Here, they identify strategy as a story, and that its 'telling' in organisations can incur considerable cost. They note that strategy is considered important and is generally thought to be influential, but by describing it as a story they question the idea that strategy is anything other than a narrative construct produced by people. By making such a statement they challenge any lingering notion that strategy is somehow a detached activity, done by rational actors utilising methods drawn from the natural sciences.

They then move their thoughts on from strategy to strategists and claim that if strategy is a story then the people who create it are storytellers. They say that strategists are 'authors of fiction' (Barry and Elmes, 1997, p. 433). By suggesting that strategy is a fiction developed by strategists, who are themselves fiction authors, Barry and Elmes are not saying that what strategists produce is false. Instead they claim they are recognising that the strategies constructed by strategists are the output of human thought and action, and not something that emerges without the active hand of one or more authors. Barry and Elmes are extremely critical of those descriptions of strategy work that ignore away the role and contribution of people who, for them, lie at the heart of all strategising. This point, of course, has been repeatedly made in this module, in Blocks 1 and 5 particularly.

They suggest the task strategists face is similar to that of the traditional fiction writers with whom we are more familiar. Strategists are subject to the same basic challenge facing other imaginative writers: they must 'develop an engaging, compelling account, one that readers can willingly buy into and implement' (Barry and Elmes, 1997, p. 433). One insight of this type of framing of strategy work is to highlight the fragile nature of strategy storytelling. No story emerges fully-formed but has to be constantly made, remade and made again, as many 'hands' contribute to its creation. Barry and Elmes identify that any strategy story that unfolds is but one of many competing alternatives that could have been told. The story that does emerge becomes the *strategy discourse*, the accepted and dominant means by which people within an organisation talk about strategy. So, the discourse itself can be a seen as a single story, or grand narrative, which is made up from and constituted by numerous smaller stories that inform it.

The three terms 'story', 'narrative' and 'discourse' are frequently used interchangeably, but we need to distinguish between them to be clear about what we are referring to. Story is best understood as consisting of a plot comprising causally related episodes culminating in a solution to a problem. So, when Barry and Elmes refer to strategy as a story they are essentially saying it is a plotline that describes a proposed solution to a problem (roughly, the future direction of the organisation). Narrative is a mode of knowing and understanding as well as a means of communicating. We make sense of things narratively ('Homo narrans') by talking with others and holding imaginary conversations in our own minds to sort through our thoughts, and we communicate with others through narrative forms in talk and writing. Stories help constitute the narrative, but the narrative consists of more than just stories. It can include signs, symbols and texts whose purpose is not necessarily to communicate a plotline, as stories do. For example, memos, reports and email communication may not necessarily tell a plotline, but could still contribute to an emerging narrative.

Discourse

Discourse is a system of statements that rules in certain ways of talking (and knowing) and rules out others. It can comprise stories and other narrative media such as emblems, pictures and gestures. To say that a strategy discourse exists is to say that within an organisation certain ways of talking and writing about strategy are acceptable, and others are not. So, viewing strategy as a discourse opens up the possibility of seeing strategy as a contested area, where certain views are favoured while others are marginalised. It is this realisation that opens up a whole new world for strategy researchers to investigate: one that casts strategists as people, and puts their humanity centre stage.

Activity 2.12: Analysing discourse

Allow **30 minutes** for this activity.

Purpose: to illustrate the concept of discourse with an example

In section 1.3, you were shown an extract from Makridakis et al. in which they discussed the possible contribution qualitative methods could make to forecasting, in their view. We reproduce the extract here:

> It is more difficult to measure the usefulness of qualitative forecasts [than of quantitative ones]. They are used mainly to provide hints, to aid the planner, and to supplement quantitative forecasts, rather than to provide a specific numerical forecast. Because of their nature and cost, they are used almost exclusively for medium- and long-range situations such as formulating strategy, developing new products and technologies, and developing long-range plans. Although doubts are often expressed about the value of qualitative forecasting, it frequently provides useful information for managers ... Qualitative methods can be used successfully in conjunction with quantitative methods in such areas as product development, capital expenditures, goal and

strategy formation, and mergers, by even medium and small organisations. Whatever the shortcomings of qualitative methods, frequently the only alternative is no forecast at all.

(1998, p. 12)

What has been said here in discourse terms? We can use a discourse perspective to develop a deeper level of understanding about what Makridakis and colleagues think and how this is influencing what they write. Please make some notes in answer to the question before reading on.

Discussion

When we presented this extract earlier, we noted that it appears a slightly 'grudging' comparison of qualitative and quantitative techniques. Let's look at this in more detail. Essentially, what we have here are proponents of the quantitative forecasting discourse attempting to consider the usefulness of a qualitative discourse. What they in fact do, in my opinion, is evaluate qualitative approaches in quantitative terms and, by doing so, find them wanting. They conduct their analysis by considering how qualitative approaches contribute to a quantitative discourse. Through this they reinforce their own preferred (quantitative) discourse and continue to marginalise the qualitative alternative. Here are some examples of what I mean:

- 'It is more difficult to measure the usefulness of qualitative forecasts' – Comment: Qualitative forecasts do not lend themselves to measurement, because they are qualitative and therefore are comprised of words. A quantitative forecast includes measurement in its discourse; qualitative forecasts do not.

- 'Although doubts are often expressed about the value of qualitative forecasting' – Comment: By whom? Other advocates of the quantitative discourse? This comment is a none-too-subtle way of saying there are doubts about qualitative forecasting (within the quantitative discourse) and bringing attention to them. Criticising the qualitative discourse is a much more comfortable position for Makridakis et al. to be in as they return to it again at the end of the quote.

- 'Whatever the shortcomings of qualitative methods, frequently the only alternative is no forecast at all' – Comment: A criticism again, but then a suggestion that even a qualitative forecast is better than nothing! My overall impression of this is that you will learn little about qualitative forecasting from authors that are so enmeshed in a quantitative discourse (the same may be true for quantitative forecasting explained by those advocating a qualitative discourse) and that although some may deny it, writing is not a neutral practice. As Makridakis et al. perhaps demonstrate, and our biases and preferences undoubtedly influence what we write.

Strategy discourse

Strategists talk, read, write and think, and through such acts strategies are created. Researchers who favour a discursive approach see language as constituting strategy, not merely reflecting it. What discourse-theorists are particularly interested in is the question of why certain ideas and views take hold within an organisation while others are side-lined. What this view highlights is that the strategies firms follow have gone through various stages of development, during which they will have been challenged, adapted, modified and re-worded, so that the result is not the inevitable outcome of conversations about strategy, but an unpredictable assemblage of ideas, thoughts and preferences. Strategies do not arrive fully-formed, but have to go through various stages of adaptation and modification, during which time some ideas take form, while others are discarded. Understanding why certain ways of speaking about strategy are acceptable, while others are not, raises the importance of power in strategy work. If we accept that power influences how strategies are formed, we also need to take on board the idea that other social qualities play their part. Identity, and legitimacy and authority (all discussed below) are also important to study if we are to deepen our knowledge of strategy.

Power

While there is a coercive aspect to some power relations, there is also a more positive and enabling contribution power makes to management work. Simply, without power nothing would get done. Clegg et al. (2006) have suggested that power is to organisational activity as oxygen is to breathing. Without it, things simply don't happen.

Power moves things along. This form of power has been called 'power to' and is generative and creative. Strategists use 'power to' acts to create strategies, to get things done. These acts can include arranging meetings and deciding who will attend, and writing reports for the senior management team.

The coercive aspect of power is referred to as 'power over' (Clegg et al., 2006) and this applies when power is exerted to get people to do something they would not otherwise do, or when actions are taken that suppress certain views or ideas in preference for others. Taking the same examples as for 'power to': 'power over' can be exerted when only those people who hold a certain view, or who will support a preferred way forward, are invited to a strategy meeting, and those that are likely to oppose this not invited. Depending on your perspective, then, separating the two kinds of power can depend on the context. 'Power over' can also be discerned in how certain reports are written, what they contain and, equally importantly, what they leave out. One of the tenets of discourse theory is that any text contains traces of the author's active hand, meaning that when people write things, like strategy documents, who writes them is important, as that person's (or group's) preferences, in 'power over' and 'power to' behaviour, will inevitably shape what is written. As we saw above, Makridakis et al.'s views on qualitative forecasting (1998) contain both their conscious and involuntary views of it.

A discursive understanding of strategy, then, raises the importance of power. It is not something that is ignored away, as in most traditional treatments of strategy. Instead, seeing strategy as discourse places it squarely at the forefront of our considerations. Questions such as 'how is power being exercised?' and 'how does the exercise of power shape what is being understood?' help us to recognise that strategy, in this sense, is a human construction. What becomes the strategy discourse is an output of power interactions, both facilitative (power to) and coercive (power over) acts performed by people as they work to accomplish their objectives. To understand how an organisation's strategy emerges, managers need to be aware of how their power-fuelled acts influence and shape what is done. Not to be aware of this would be like doctors trying to understand breathing while ignoring the contribution of oxygen. Their understanding is only superficial if they do not include this vital element.

Identity

Identity in this context refers to self-image, which includes how we see ourselves and how we would like others to see us. Also, it refers to individual and group or organisational identity. How we see ourselves and how we would like others to see us influences what we do, our praxis in short (Whittington, 2006, p. 11). We like to think that we act in accordance with our own self-perceptions, so understanding these is important if we are to deepen our knowledge of how and why things are done. Alterity is a related concept to identity and is the term used to describe what we are not. So, if identity is about our self-image, alterity refers to our image(s) of what we are not. Members of a senior management team will have individual identities as people, but will also have a collective identity which is comprised of shared aspects of their individual identities. This shared identity will also display what they are not – their alterity.

Does identity matter? Yes, discourse scholars would say, because it helps define the limits of a discourse. It is unlikely that issues that challenge an identity will be allowed to influence the discourse. An example of this could be where a university senate, the supreme academic body within a university, is asked to consider or take on board a proposal that runs counter to the identities, both individual and collective, of its members. Members of a senate that have built their identity on research excellence are unlikely to support a proposal for change in the university's organisation or systems that they see as incompatible with the continuing prioritisation and support of research.

A strategy discourse, then, is constructed around the identities of those who constitute it. Just as members of a university senate are likely to act in ways that they see as compatible with that role, so strategists are likely to act in ways that affirm their identity as strategists. Strategists are unlikely to act in ways that challenge their own self-image. For many years, students of strategy have been told that strategy is a rational pursuit that involves the key elements of analysis, choice and implementation – indeed, this module's structure reflects this sequence in the relationship of Blocks 2, 3 and 5. Therefore, to act like strategists, in the minds of most students, is to undertake tasks commensurate with these activities. Not to do so would mean they were not assuming the identity of 'strategist'.

In organisations, understanding the dominant collective identity is important if a strategy discourse is to take hold. If a discourse challenges this identity for example, a finance-oriented discourse within an engineering-dominated firm, it is unlikely to be accepted. To have their discourse take hold, strategists within such a firm would have to couch their argument in engineering terms for it to stand any chance of being accepted.

Legitimacy and authority

These two concepts are usually taken hand-in-hand, but are slightly different and a distinction between them needs to be made. Authority is generally used in hierarchical terms, so those higher up in an organisation's hierarchy are usually felt to have more authority than those lower down. Legitimacy, on the other hand, may have less to do with hierarchy and be more concerned with reputation and having the 'right' to speak knowledgeably about a topic. It can be won through experience; having worked on a particular issue for a significant amount of time. For example, a front-of-house receptionist can speak with legitimacy about the checking-in and checking-out processes in a hotel, because he or she is involved in them on a daily basis, but may have little authority. In contrast, a hotel general manager may have greater authority, but their legitimacy to speak knowledgeably about such processes may be limited because of their other duties.

To develop our understanding about how discourses emerge, legitimacy and authority are key concepts. Also, in contrast to the hotel example above, strategy practitioners discussed in Block 5 included external actors, as well as those internal to the organisation. This is important because external actors in the guise of strategy consultants, for example, are assigned both legitimacy and authority. As was shown in Block 5, what they say and do affects how strategy within organisations is conceptualised. When strategy consultants interact with a client they bring with them a stock of legitimacy that means they are listened to and taken account of. Indeed, recent research on the reasons why management consultancy firms are engaged by clients suggests that sometimes the legitimacy they bring with them to a project is considered more important than any particular knowledge or skills they may impart (Wright, 2008). So, as far as the strategy discourse is concerned, internal and external actors influence its form. By considering issues of authority and legitimacy, we can get a better understanding of how those in authority use this to shape the discourse, and how legitimate actors ensure their voice is heard. For a strategy discourse to take hold within an organisation it must be authoritative; it must be seen by those it seeks to influence as being entitled to their acceptance. This is achieved, in part, through being perceived as legitimate, meaning it comes from a legitimate source or sources. When discourses fail to convince it could be because they fail to carry sufficient authority and legitimacy among their target audience.

Activity 2.13: Three vignettes illustrating strategy as discourse

Allow **60 minutes** for this activity.

Purpose: to explore how strategy discourse is created, with particular reference to the impact of power, identity, authority and legitimacy

What follows are three brief vignettes (short word pictures depicting an evocative description, account or episode) taken from ongoing research that one of the authors of this block is engaged in (a study of an organisation working with external strategy consultants). As is conventional, the organisation is anonymised in the vignettes – simply referred to as 'client'. Any direct quotations are taken from interviews conducted as part of the research. The vignettes offer small insights into how the strategy discourse is created, and are designed to illustrate how the issues of power, identity, authority and legitimacy impact upon how the strategy discourse materialises in organisations. Read through the extracts and then reflect on what the pertinent issues are; a discussion follows at the end that highlights some of the main insights to be drawn from the vignettes.

Vignette 1

Consultants were working with a client in order to produce a strategy in document form. The client had expressed the need to ensure the process was highly consultative, stressing the need for staff within the firm to feel involved, and for stakeholders outside the organisation to believe their views mattered and were taken account of. To achieve this, the strategy-making process involved eight workshops, divided into three sets: 'exploring the drivers', 'building up strategic insight' and 'identifying goals and indicators'. The second set of these, 'building up strategic insight', required the consultants to write a report on their findings. This report was intended to be based on the views of the workshop attendees, so they were invited to express their ideas. One of the client's internal strategists observed this and commented on how the consultants rephrased the words of the attendees back to them 'in a slightly different way, and then that is captured, and then that's interpreted. So, they really control how it's written'. After the report was drafted, the consultants sent it to the client's internal strategists for comment, which they did. When asked about their role in this process during an interview, one of the consultants asserted, 'We're just the blank surface for the process'. However, the second consultant then related an example of how they had responded to some of the comments by the client, 'There are times when [client] have come back to us and said, "Actually, we don't agree that's right". And we, as the authors, if you like, have gone back to them and said, "Well, actually, let's just talk through why we think it's important that that piece stays as it is"'.

Exercise 1

Having read through Vignette 1, identify the power issues you can discern. It may help to think of the distinction between 'power to' and 'power over' explained above.

 Vignette 2

At the end of the strategy-making process referred to in Vignette 1, the client asked for a close-down meeting with the consultants to review what had happened. Prior to the meeting, the client's internal strategists got together to discuss what they wanted from the meeting. The lead strategist eventually wrote down four questions on the meeting-room whiteboard around which he wanted the discussion to focus:

- How [client's] experience compares with the consultants' experiences elsewhere?

- How [client's] experience of working with the consultants compares with the experience of other clients working with them?

- What could we [client] have done better?

- Future work?

The first two points will be the focus of this vignette as they reveal something about what were the chief concerns at the forefront of the strategists' minds. Remember, this was a close-down meeting, therefore the consultancy intervention had ended, so the agenda represents the post-strategy-making concerns of the client's strategists. During the meeting, the lead internal strategist spent some time asking how the consultants' experience with them compared with their experiences with other similar clients. The consultants responded by assuring the meeting that this organisation had worked more effectively with the consultants than some of their other clients. This, as you can imagine, went down quite well with the client's internal strategists.

Exercise 2

Looking at the first two points on the agenda, what does this tell us about the identity of the client's strategists? What appears to be the main concern of the client's strategists regarding their own self-image and how they would like others to see them?

Vignette 3

While the Stage Two workshops were taking place (referred to in Vignette 1), the client organisation's chief executive officer (CEO) approached the lead internal strategist and presented him with a list of strategic goals he had produced with the intention that these be accepted as the goals that would appear in the final strategy document. The CEO's list had been developed outside of the agreed process. The original process, agreed between the client and consultants, had designated the stage three workshops as the place where the goals would be created, so by producing the goals when he did, the CEO was effectively attempting to subvert this. The lead internal strategist had to respond to the CEO's efforts. He did this by producing his own set of goals, which were drawn from the work that was coming out of the Stage Two workshops. A period of negotiation then took place between the CEO, his office and the internal strategy unit. The lead internal strategist's list of goals was eventually accepted by CEO. The third stage of workshops, although unnecessary now that strategy goals had been identified, still went ahead and the participants in these spoke favourably about their experiences.

Exercise 3

Analyse Vignette 3 and identify the authority and legitimacy issues it contains. How did the actors concerned use their authority and legitimacy in their attempts to significantly affect the strategy discourse?

Discussion

Vignette 1 demonstrates how subtle uses of 'power over' influences what becomes accepted as 'the way we talk about strategy around here'. The client's internal strategist, in describing how the consultants rephrase an expression back to the speaker, slightly changing it, identify 'power over' behaviour in action. The consultants, in effect, have the power to interpret what is being said in a way that they find acceptable and that fits in with their conception of strategy. An argument could also be made to suggest that what the consultants did was also a practical 'power to' activity, in that their rephrasing is necessary to progress the workshop. The multiple voices in a workshop setting need to be unified in some sense, or they remain separate voices relating alternative stories. The second part of this vignette is perhaps more revealing, as we have a consultant claiming their role in writing a report is neutral and value-free; therefore, he conceptualises this role in 'power to' terms. This is then challenged when the other consultant relates an example of how they use their authorial power ('power over') in arguing for their text to remain as they would prefer. What we get here is an everyday example of strategists, including consultants, negotiating between themselves to reach an acceptable view of what a strategy text should contain.

Vignette 2 focuses on identity. The first two agenda items highlight how the client's internal strategists are constructing their image of themselves as competent strategists based on how they perform when compared with their peers. They seek from the consultants affirmation of their competency. The key here though, is that their image of themselves as competent strategists is based not so much on their achievements, but on the views of an authoritative source, the consultants, who have broad experience of strategy making in multiple organisations.

Vignette 3 relates an intervention by a CEO that threatened to derail the strategy-making process agreed between consultants and their client. Conventionally, it might be assumed that authority rested with the CEO to impose his views onto a strategy process, significantly affecting the discourse. However, in this instance, although the lead internal strategist possessed less authority than the CEO, he had greater legitimacy. The negotiations that took place between the CEO and the strategy unit can be framed as a discussion between authority and legitimacy. The triumph of legitimacy over authority in this example suggests that it is most important for any strategy discourse to be seen as legitimate. Had authority won out and the CEO been successful in imposing his will (itself a clear example of 'power over' activity), this may have resulted in the discourse lacking credibility because of the absence of legitimacy. A discredited discourse is unlikely to take hold and become adopted by the people at whom it is aimed.

What promise does viewing strategy as a discourse hold?

How might viewing strategy as discourse help us to understand it better and do it more effectively? Having briefly looked through the ideas underpinning the view that strategy is best viewed as a discourse, we will now try to answer the 'so what?' question in a series of points. These points highlight the key contribution strategy from a discursive perspective brings to our knowledge of strategy. In a way they are the things that distinguish this view from others and it is this distinction where the contribution lies.

- Replacing the 'Homo economicus' view of human beings with 'Homo narrans' (Fisher, 1984), suggests that people make sense of their organisational lives through constructing and telling stories. Firms in this view are complex sites of storytelling, where individuals constantly create stories about their lives that mingle with other stories created by their colleagues. Organising, in these terms, comes together when stories collide and new stories emerge. This approach to understanding strategy highlights the significance of strategists to an organisation's concept of strategy. Who they are, what their backgrounds are, who they talk to, and what ambitions they hold will all shape the type of strategy discourses they see as reasonable and appropriate.

- The practice-based research this inspires does not seek to make grand, generalisable statements about strategy, but makes claims about its usefulness based on limited but revealing insights from particular cases. A practice-research sensibility brings contextual nuance to the surface, and through doing so enriches our understanding of how strategy work is and should be done.

- We have seen that the idea of strategy as a story has been around for a number of years (Barry and Elmes, 1997); it is not just some recent fad or fashion. If strategy is a story, strategists are storytellers, authors of fictions, and they face the same challenge as traditional fiction authors. They work at developing a story of strategy that is engaging and compelling, and one people can believe in. Stories within organisations are created by people, who will have preferences, motivations and biases that inevitably inform what they do. Claims towards objectivity, neutrality and detachment should therefore be questioned, and the assumptions that underpin them surfaced, so that these can be productively challenged. Scenario planning, as outlined in Unit 1, may be one approach that helps to do this.

- Strategy as a discourse integrates story and narrative. This view sees strategy as narrated (talked, written, thought about and read) into being. When individuals talk about strategy within a firm, they are not representing it, but are creating it through their talk, so strategy is never static but always unfolding through the conversations generated by it. A discourse-based view of strategy explains why some ways of talking about strategy are deemed acceptable and others are marginalised. Senior managers, middle managers and others, if they wish to be heard, need to adopt the dominant discourse, otherwise their contribution may be marginalised.

- Power and strategy are inexorably intertwined. Without power, strategy could not exist, but power shapes what is seen as strategy in multiple ways. 'Power over' can be seen as largely coercive – a way to get others to do something they might not do by choice. Our vignettes in Activity 2.13 demonstrate that frequently its use is more subtle than that. 'Power to' acknowledges the positive, generative role of power in everyday organising and the vignettes highlight how people use this to progress strategy work. Organisations that rely excessively on 'power over' may suffer, in that strategies imposed may be ignored by middle managers. 'Power to' organisations, however, will be characterised as more open, and may be able to undertake strategic action more effectively.

- Identity is important for understanding strategy in two key ways. First, through the self-images of the strategists themselves and, second, through the identities of the senior managers, middle managers and general workforce in terms of how acceptable to their self-image any strategy will be. Strategists, like most of us, want to appear competent and like their peers, only perhaps a bit better! Strategists that have received some form of graduate or postgraduate education can draw from their studies to reinforce their identities as strategists. The strategies produced need to align with the self-image of the wider constituency they are aimed at, or they are likely to be seen as lacking credibility and the intended discourse will not take hold.

- Legitimacy and authority are related but distinct terms that help us understand why some actions are accepted while others are challenged. Vignette 3 in Activity 2.13 demonstrated that attempts by an authoritative source to impose their will on a discourse are not always successful and perhaps legitimacy is more important than authority. In the context of strategy authority and legitimacy can come from individuals and organisations external to the focus organisations. As discussed in Block 5, strategy consultants have an increasing presence in much strategy work. Shareholders and other stakeholders (discussed in Block 2) may also influence how the strategy discourse emerges. Strategies and strategic action that are not perceived under the cloak of legitimacy are unlikely to take hold. This highlights for organisations the importance of strategies being viewed as legitimate for them to be adopted. When this is not the case, organisations may be tempted to use greater authority to impose them on a reluctant workforce. Rather, they should work to establish that missing legitimacy.

2.3: Strategy and critical management studies

Our accounts of complexity theory and discourse have offered alternative and, to some extent, complementary perspectives on strategy to those we have encountered already. Discourse theory reveals how strategists play language games to rule in some versions of strategy and rule out others in specific organisational contexts, and more widely in terms of what it means to be a strategist professionally (or, indeed, academically). Discourse can therefore be seen to be a 'critical' perspective in a way that complexity theory is not. Complexity theory exposes the workings of strategy as a 'natural' phenomenon obeying principles similar to those at work in other complex adaptive systems in nature. But discourse theory argues that strategy is very much a cultural construct rather than a natural phenomenon – with boundaries set by powerful actors to advance their interests and goals at the expense of less powerful ones. This allows us to look at strategy more critically, to make sense of it not necessarily as driven by considered decisions in the best interests of the organisation, or as some kind of naturally-emerging process, but as the result of an ongoing power struggle.

This section develops the idea of taking a critical perspective on strategy as a concept and practice in itself, rather than using critical thinking to interrogate aspects of it as has been our practice in the module to this point.

Management: innocent or ideological?

Throughout this module we have encouraged you to think critically about the concepts and models we have introduced in order to avoid the danger of accepting them as universally applicable or reliable across all circumstances. We have underlined the importance of a positively critical approach to articles and readings in order to consider the context in which they were written and the perspectives they represent.

As we approach the end of the module, it is a good opportunity to take account of an approach to studying management that moves being critical to a more global level (and, as ever, to invite you to be critical of this approach as well). To this point in our studies we have referred to critical thinking in the context of various aspects of studying management. However, what if we were to be critical of the whole idea of management itself – to 'look behind' it, and ask in whose interests it acts or what effect it has on society or the environment? You may have found yourself beginning to do this already, or perhaps you have come to the conclusion that the relevance of critical thinking is confined to helping us be better managers within the existing framework (or paradigm) of management. In one sense, you can argue that management is an innocent tool. Management itself has no moral content: what matters is what you do with it. Or, alternatively, you might argue that such a view of management risks ignoring the ideology that underlies it (and which management arguably reinforces).

Put simply, ideology can be defined as a system of ideas that underlies political or social action, or, more particularly, which legitimates the subordination of one group in society to another. So you could argue that the very idea of management itself is based on the assumption that one group in society (managers) have legitimate power over one or more other groups (the managed – be they employees, suppliers, customers or stakeholders). Questioning this assumption may strike you as absurd or affected – after all, that is just the way things are. You have to have management or things would not happen (a bit like our justification of power in the previous section discussing discourse). But critics of ideology (following Marx and Engels' *The German Ideology* written in the 1840s) point out that ideology presents a picture of the world that looks 'natural' but which invariably works in favour of the most powerful elements of society (Marx and Engels, 1974). Ideology is therefore, by definition, partial rather than representative of the interests of humanity as a whole. So the argument that management is only natural may ignore a rather less 'natural' state of affairs.

You don't have to be anti-capitalist or anti-business to find some value in this critical approach – although how convincing you find it will probably depend on how it fits into your general view of the world. By now in your studies, especially your study of strategy in this module, you will appreciate that what you regard as valid knowledge (your epistemology, to repeat the term used in the previous section) depends on your deep-seated convictions about how the world works (your ontology). To pick an example from strategy, how convincing you find the 'knowledge' produced about strategy by the positioning school depends on what you believe about 'reality' as far as the nature of the industry environment is concerned. A prominent criticism of the positioning school is that the nature of reality in the environment is so fast-moving as to be impossible to pin down in the way required by Porter's model.

In the context of the present discussion, if your view of the nature of social reality is that it consists of a number of elements struggling with each other for power (what is known broadly in sociology as 'conflict theory') then you are more likely to accept the critical approach we are outlining here. If, on the other hand, your view of social reality sees it as a complicated, self-regulating and ultimately consensual system (known broadly as 'functionalism' in sociology) then you are more likely to see management as a neutral, technical activity that fulfils a necessary social function, and regard critical management studies as, at best, an interesting but unconvincing intellectual backwater, or, at worst, a biased irrelevance.

Whatever your personal stance, it is worth taking account of critical management studies as it frames the subject of strategy. It is a growing area of research interest academically, and can be argued to reflect concerns which are representative of contemporary workers and customers – for example, the lack of 'trust' of major institutions which many commentators see as endemic in today's society (O'Neill, 2002).

The development of critical management studies

Critical management studies is an evolving field. A 2007 article describes it as:

> a range of alternatives to mainstream management theory with a view to radically transforming management practice. The common core is deep skepticism regarding the moral defensibility and the social and ecological sustainability of prevailing conceptions and forms of management and organisations. [Critical management studies'] motivating concern is neither the personal failures of individual managers nor the poor management of specific firms, but the social injustice and environmental destructiveness that these managers serve and reproduce.

(Adler et al., 2007, p. 119)

This view of management sees it as far from an innocent tool. Instead it argues that management in organisations is rendered necessary by (and contributes to) existing divisions in society between 'blue collar' and 'white collar' workers, owners and employees, and permanent staff and part-time or contract workers. Management presides over processes that emphasise profit over all else as in the Classical school of strategy

(Whittington, 2001). All too often, this results in waste, environmental degradation and exploitation.

This may seem a bizarre position to us as students of management. We are used to conceiving of management as precisely the opposite of wasteful. Good management provides meaningful and purposive work for individuals, and confers benefits on wider society through its role in the production and provision of goods and services. But even capitalism's staunchest defenders acknowledge that shareholder interests come before those of other stakeholders. Non-profit management pursues targets other than profit and therefore might be seen as more accountable (for example, targets may be the result of democratic decisions). But distortion is possible because of short-term political imperatives, and the charges of social divisiveness and negative environmental impact apply to all sectors.

A more questioning attitude to management has led to a more questioning attitude to management education. The late Sumantra Ghoshal (1948–2004), of the London Business School, struck a chord around the world in a posthumously published article castigating business schools for ignoring ethics in their teaching:

> Academic research related to the conduct of business and management has had some very significant and negative influences on the practice of management … by propagating ideologically inspired amoral theories, business schools have actively freed their students from any sense of moral responsibility.

> (Ghoshal, 2005, p. 76, cited by Adler et al., 2007, p.121)

Critical management studies advocates a less 'partial' approach to management, based on individual autonomy and collective cooperation. How realistic such ideals are is open to question, but – as Ghoshal demonstrates – concern about the alternative of 'business as usual' is now reaching mainstream thinking.

As articulated by two of its pioneers, Alvesson and Willmott (the authors of Reading 19), critical management studies draws its inspiration from a body of thought called critical theory. Critical theory was developed in the first half of the twentieth century by a group of social researchers usually referred to as the Frankfurt School. Critical of the anti-democratic trends of 1930s German society, they were equally scathing about the version of democracy they found in America having fled there from the Nazis – particularly the way in which, as they saw it, the masses were held in thrall to unthinking consumerism by mainstream popular culture. Critical theory proposed a radical critique of consumer society, aspiring instead to an ideal society of autonomous individuals united to control their own destiny. Critical theory aimed at emancipating people from what it saw as oppressive (and unnecessary) social constraints – and critical management studies harbours the same idealistic ambition. Having fallen out of fashion in the 1980s (replaced by more 'active' views of individuals in society), critical theory is regaining ground in the early twenty-first century because of renewed concerns about the relative power of citizens and corporate/political interests in an unstable world (*In Our Time*, 2010).

As a framework for researchers taking a critical perspective on management, critical theory has been augmented by more recent influences including feminism (concerned at how accepted notions of management perpetuate male domination in society), environmentalism (pointing to the unacknowledged costs of management in the environmental degradation which often accompanies its practice) and postmodernism (questioning all kinds of hierarchy and claims to truth). Since the 1990s, critical management research has been gathering momentum in business schools in specialisms such as human resource management, finance, operational research and marketing (Saren et al., 2007). As we have seen in the previous section, there are clear links between 'strategy as practice' research and critical interest in power, authority and legitimacy. Activity 2.14 centres on a reading that sets out some critical perspectives with specific relevance to strategy. The reading is extracted from the 2012 second edition of a book first published in 1996 – one of the first to set out a critical agenda for management research. Its authors, Alvesson and Willmott are still commited to critical theory (referred to in the reading as 'CT') as their theoretical underpinning, and have left the section on strategy virtually unchanged. One of the questions to keep in your mind as you read it is: to what extent have things changed in management since it was originally published in 1996?

Activity 2.14: Critical theory and strategic management

Allow **90 minutes** for this activity, including 30 minutes for participation in your TGF discussion.

Purpose: to relate questions about strategy to critical management studies

Please turn to Reading 19, an extract from *Making sense of management* by Alvesson and Willmott. We hope that by now many of the authorities cited and arguments described in the early part of the extract will be familiar to you from your work on this module. Study the extract and make brief notes in answer to the following questions:

- What do the authors suggest can be revealed by asking questions about the 'processes that produce the rules by which an "organisation" is managed and judged?'

- What do the authors see as the limitations of orthodox and processual approaches to analysing strategic management?

- The authors imply that less 'strategy talk' might be a good idea. Why?

- Why is concentration a problem as understood by the authors?

- What positive alternative to orthodox strategy do the authors propose?

Discussion

Here are some notes in answer to these points against which you can compare yours.

- Questioning the production of criteria against which organisations are managed and judged reveals the operation of power. The authors argue that senior managers' self-interest is expressed through such rules, and that real strategic choice is constrained as a result. As long as the power relations remain unchanged, strategy is unlikely to change either.

- The problem with orthodox and processual approaches as argued here is that they stop short of revealing strategy's place in the system of domination by some groups in society of others. In particular, by stressing a technical rational approach to decision making in organisations, orthodox approaches remove the possibility of a more inclusive, democratic way of working. Even processual ways of understanding strategic decision making (e.g. incrementalism) focus on detail rather than the wider power relations, which frame strategy.

- Strategy talk (a similar idea to 'strategy as discourse') is seen by Alvesson and Willmott as colonising (i.e. 'taking over') other areas of activity and thought. We might think this is trivial, or even amusing (as in the equation of 'strategic' with 'big') but it has a political effect. It closes down debate by reminding us that strategy is more important than other ways of looking at the world; it confirms the status of 'strategists' and it has sexist overtones. It thus has an effect on the 'ideational world' (how we conceive of things through generating ideas) and contributes to 'hegemony' about strategy's importance ('hegemony' means the accepted dominance of a particular way of thinking).

- Concentration of ownership of organisations, particularly those in areas like public relations, advertising or media, may be good business sense because it reduces competition, but is bad for society because it reduces diversity. The authors do not mention the checks and balances provided by regulation in this area (competition law in the UK and Europe, also known as 'anti-trust' in the US). But they indicate how the 'strategic' aim of triumphing over the competition may be seen to be at odds with social welfare in general, and particularly in terms of its environmental impact.

- The general thrust of the last section of the extract is that wider participation in strategic decision making, supported by open communication processes which allow question and reconsideration, is a desirable alternative to the current monopoly of decision-making power by senior management. In particular, the authors conclude that critical theory would require not only participation in decision making, but also in the establishment of appropriately wide goals (reflecting social priorities as well as business ones). You may feel that elements of such processes are increasingly at work through organisations' attention to stakeholder analysis and CSR, or, alternatively, that such initiatives only pay lip service to social goals. Or, indeed, you may concur with Milton Friedman's much-cited view that the only social responsibility of business is to increase its profits (Friedman, 1970).

There's a lot to think about in this reading, so we hope you will take plenty of ideas with you to the TGF as you continue your reflections online. How relevant do you think Alvesson and Willmott's ideas are to the contemporary world of organisations? In particular, how relevant are their ideas to your own professional or personal context?

Criticising critical management studies

One problem with this approach to management and strategy is that it does not appear to have much to say of immediate practical use to managers, other than that they are involved in oppressive structures. Indeed, one of the most common objections to critical theory in general has been that it does not engage with praxis, preferring to limit itself to criticising things as they are against an idealised version of how they might be (Bradshaw and Fuat Firat, 2007).

Critical management researchers might reply to this objection that there is a difference between 'knowledge of' and 'knowledge for' management. If your interest as a student or researcher is in the subject of business for its own sake (in the same way as you might be interested in studying psychology or history) it might not matter greatly to you if the 'knowledge of' management on which you choose to focus is of immediate practical use. It may have practical application in a future combination with other knowledge, or it may help you think in broader terms about practical issues, but you do not expect it immediately to make you a better manager in the technical sense. Indeed, too exclusive a concentration on technical matters to the exclusion of the wider context of management is one of the things to which critical management studies objects. If, on the other hand, your interest in studying or researching business is to find more effective ways of managing (i.e. 'knowledge for' management), then you may well be frustrated with an approach that fails to deliver anything much in answer to the 'so what?' question as it might be asked by a practitioner.

Many students of business studies, perhaps yourself included, are motivated by the opportunity to develop practical, 'technical' skills, as well as by the intrinsic interest of the subject itself – and, typically for a business school, the learning outcomes of this module reflect this. So perhaps the 'knowledge for' and 'knowledge of' distinction is not an entirely realistic one. Certainly one of the justifications for studying strategy is that it is an intensely practical subject – but that is also part of what makes it interesting in its own right.

Furthermore, some would argue that it is perfectly feasible to combine the aim of successful strategy from a shareholder point of view with wider societal values. Critical management studies regards this position with suspicion, seeing corporate social responsibility (CSR) as insufficiently systemic to make much impact on the underlying structures of power and domination within which management operates. But, as Alvesson and Willmott argue (with reference to their own critical-theory-informed brand of critical management), their intention is not 'inherently or relentlessly "anti-management"'. Rather, it is to reframe management (and therefore strategy as well) positively as 'a collective task concerned with the identification and realization, through processes of critical self-reflection, of alternative values and practices that are humanly (and ecologically) more fulfilling and less degrading' (Reading 19).

We began this brief introduction to critical management studies by arguing that it involved being critical in a much wider, systemic sense than the way in which we have been using the term up to this point. However, Alvesson and Willmott's emphasis on processes of 'critical self-reflection' suggests that such criticality has its roots in the personal reflectiveness of the individual manager, not taking the circumstances and processes of everyday managerial life at face value but looking behind them and questioning them in search of better alternatives (reflecting a wider range of priorities than those usually stressed in strategic thinking). From that point of view, perhaps critical management studies represents more continuity than is at first apparent with some of the more orthodox ideas it finds wanting.

CSR as a source of competitive advantage

Michael Porter, whose work from the 1980s and 1990s has made such an important contribution to strategy theory and practice, has turned his attention more recently to the role of strategy in society. You will recall that one of the characteristics of the Classical school of strategy, according to Whittington (2001) is that it sees the business of business as making profit rather than 'doing good' in society. Porter's interest in strategy for non-profit organisations, such as charities and healthcare providers, in the twenty-first century would appear to be a development away from this basic position. However (unlike critical management theorists), Porter sees no conflict between the interests of profit-oriented business and those of society at large. He argues that a healthy society needs a buoyant business sector, and vice versa. In a 2006 article, Porter and his co-author, strategy consultant Mark Kramer, note the rapid growth in CSR initiatives, but suggest that most are misguided: 'First, they pit business against society, when clearly the two are interdependent. Second, they pressure companies to think of corporate social responsibility in generic ways instead of in the way most appropriate to each firm's strategy' (Porter and Kramer, 2006, p. 78).

Porter and Kramer divide what they see as misguided arguments for CSR into four main themes.

- First, the idea that businesses should act morally simply because it is the right thing to do. On the face of it, it is hard to argue with this principle. However, Porter and Kramer argue that clear ideas of right and wrong are not always easy to reconcile with the number of conflicting priorities that companies face. Which is the more ethical course of action, for example: creating jobs by building a new factory in an area of low employment, or preserving a habitat which supports rare wildlife? Both these choices could be the opposite side of the same coin – so it is hard to see how moral value alone can offer a simple guide to CSR.

- Second, the idea of 'sustainability' as a principle. Porter and Kramer cite the definition offered by the former Norwegian Prime Minister Gro Harlem Brundtland: 'Meeting the needs of the present without compromising the ability of future generations to meet their own needs' (2006, p. 81). Again, a principle from which it would be hard to dissent. Sustainability tends to involve reducing waste, and thus costs. Porter and Kramer cite examples of this approvingly, for instance, an energy-reduction initiative by DuPont, which saved the company $2 billion over 25 years. However, unless it has clear cost-saving benefits, they argue, sustainability is too vague a notion on which to build a CSR strategy as its sole platform.

- License to operate is the third generic argument Porter and Kramer cite for CSR. This is the idea that stakeholders, such as citizens and government, give companies 'permission' to do what they do. Our account of stakeholders in Block 2 underlined the importance of managing them appropriately as part of the business environment. CSR activity of some sort may be a way of doing this, depending on the circumstances, but seeing license to operate as the foundation of your CSR strategy risks ceding control of an important part of your strategic direction to others, which negates the concept of having a strategy in the first place. Furthermore, the most salient stakeholders (sometimes just those who are loudest) may not be the most important in the long run.

- Finally, Porter and Kramer mention reputation as a justification often given for CSR. There is little doubt that it can improve image, boost morale, even help sustain share prices. But focusing too exclusively on the benefits to reputation risks a CSR strategy descending into short-term public relations rather than strategically based long-term action for the joint good of business and society.

These four arguments are common justifications for CSR, but all are flawed, according to Porter and Kramer, because they concentrate on what divides business and society rather than what they have in common. They explain:

> The fact is, the prevailing approaches to CSR are so fragmented and so disconnected from business and strategy as to obscure many of the greatest opportunities for companies to benefit society. If, instead, corporations were to analyze their prospects for social responsibility using the same frameworks that guide their core business choices, they would discover that CSR can be much more than a cost, a constraint, or a charitable deed – it can be a source of opportunity, innovation, and competitive advantage.

(Porter and Kramer, 2006, p. 80)

This might sound as if Porter and Kramer are too interested in the benefits to the organisation from CSR, but their argument is that a well-chosen programme of CSR creates good for society as well as the originating organisation.

As you might expect from your knowledge of Porter's previous work, Porter and Kramer urge organisations to approach CSR as they would strategy in general. It requires a clear decision to position the organisation in a way that sets it apart distinctively from the competition, doing something that reflects and reinforces its chosen position in the market. There are plenty of worthy causes out there, Porter and Kramer acknowledge, and businesses cannot hope to support them all. Instead of wasting effort on disjointed and short-term activities (however socially responsible) companies should carefully select the most strategically appropriate activity and concentrate on that.

The argument supporting Porter and Kramer's position on CSR as something that needs to create joint value is all very well but what practical advice can they offer managers to help position their CSR strategies appropriately? This part of their article builds on two models which you encountered in Block 2 – the value chain and the diamond framework. Porter and Kramer argue that practically every activity in an organisation's value chain creates some kind of social impact where it takes place. Such impacts can be positive, such as employment opportunities, or negative, such as noise or emissions. Just as in its commercial application, the value chain can be used to understand and identify opportunities to increase CSR value for both the company and its stakeholders – either by enhancing positive impact (like a company investing in local education where it recruits workers) or mitigating negative impact (such as supporting a conservation programme in an area where it creates noise or pollution).

The value chain helps identify the impact of the organisation on its environment. The diamond framework, on the other hand, helps identify the impact of its environment on the organisation. External circumstances impact on organisations from the four elements of the diamond framework which together create what Porter and Kramer term 'the competitive context' (2006, p. 84). This context can support or constrain strategy, again providing the inspiration for an appropriate CSR programme. As you will recall from Figure 3.1 in Block 2 Unit 3 (reproduced below as Figure 2.4) the diamond framework covers four elements:

- Factor conditions – the availability of business input such as human resources, materials or transport infrastructure. Strategic CSR might take the form of a company working with local producers in the developing world to increase the efficiency, and thus the returns, of their farming activity.

- Structure of firms and rivalry – boosted in some geographical locations by government policies to encourage investment or prevent corruption. Strategic CSR in this context might cover investment in local infrastructure, such as schools or hospitals, to help the development of stable communities where a company has markets or factories.

- Demand conditions – the strength and sophistication of demand from consumers and organisational buyers. For example, a company like American Express, much of whose business depends on travel and entertainment, might support an arts organisation like an opera or dance company, whose success would stimulate tourism and cultural activity in a particular location.

- Related and supporting industries – are there 'clusters' of related support industries providing services and technology? Strategic CSR here, and in the previous category of 'demand conditions', might involve investment in local employment and education in order to create better prospects for local economic development.

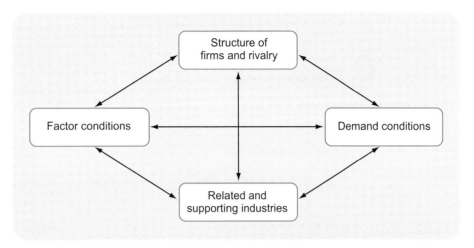

Figure 2.4 Porter's diamond of national advantage framework (Source: Porter, 1990, p. 77)

Porter and Kramer argue that these elements, the value chain and 'competitive context' can help the organisation determine a CSR strategy that promises to maximise both social and business benefits. 'The essential test that should guide CSR is not whether a cause is worthy but whether it presents an opportunity to create shared value – that is, a meaningful benefit for society that is also valuable to the business' (Porter and Kramer, 2006, p. 84). CSR policy can mitigate adverse local impacts from the value chain, rendering them more effective and reducing costs. Or it can enhance an aspect of the 'competitive context' to the organisation's advantage as well as that of the community in which it is working. Such activity acknowledges that there are limits to what individual businesses can do to enhance social welfare, but suggests that there is not necessarily a contradiction between the welfare of business and that of society. Recognising this mutuality of interest is the key to maximise the benefits for both: 'No social program can rival the business sector when it comes to creating the jobs, wealth, and innovation that improve standards of living and social conditions over time' (Porter and Kramer, 2006, p. 83).

Activity 2.15: Comparing CSR programmes

Allow **30 minutes** for this activity.

Purpose: to consolidate your understanding of Porter and Kramer's (2006) linkage between competitive advantage and CSR.

Read the following two examples of CSR in action. The first is from the UK high street retailer Boots (since 2006, part of the international Alliance Boots group). It is an extract from its CSR report for 2012–13. The second is from Salesforce.com, a global business services firm which has established a foundation (Salesforce.com Foundation) to carry out and encourage charitable work. Its website invites other organisations to 'take the 1/1/1 pledge' – the principle being that Salesforce.com devotes one per cent of employee time to volunteering each year, donates one per cent of its products (by value, it would appear) to non-profits each year, either in kind or by offering discounts, and donates one per cent of its equity value each year to good causes, mainly led by employee suggestions. Taking into account Porter and Kramer's advice about maximising shared value, which approach to CSR do you think is likely to be more effective and why?

Example 1: Boots

Our CSR mission and purpose

'To be the UK's most socially responsible retailer in the health and beauty market.'

We will do this by:

- improving the health of our customers and their communities

- protecting the environment

- leading the development of sustainable products

- placing our customers and colleagues at the heart of our business.

Throughout our 160 year history, you will find many examples of responsible business practice and the active role that Boots UK has played in helping to build healthy and more sustainable communities.

Today, issues such as climate change, resource scarcity, youth unemployment and a growing focus on town centres that recognises their role in providing community cohesion and identity, are just a few examples of the need for a more joined up, collaborative approach between many stakeholders if we are to make urgent progress.

The importance of robust governance and operational management of these issues has never been more important and, of course, our customers expect nothing less.

Our CSR scorecard

Informed by ongoing consultation and dialogue with an extensive network of key stakeholders, our strategy is shaped by a well-established, best practice scorecard model for CSR management and reporting covering four key areas; community, environment, marketplace and workplace. Each priority work stream within the scorecard has a long-term plan with assigned accountability and responsibility for delivery, together with targets and milestones against which performance is monitored and reported.

We review the priorities that make up our scorecard regularly in order to ensure that they best reflect current issues, meet the needs of our stakeholders, and are fully aligned to our business strategy, as well as ensuring our efforts meet with Alliance Boots overall priorities.

Progress is reported regularly to the Boots UK executive team and to the Alliance Boots social responsibilities committee.

(Source: Boots UK, 2013)

Example 2: Salesforce.com

The Salesforce.com Foundation is based on a simple idea: Leverage salesforce.com's people, technology, and resources to help improve communities around the world. We call this integrated philanthropic approach the 1/1/1 model.

What if all companies integrated giving back into their business models?

Take the 1/1/1 Pledge

The 1/1/1 Pledge is an effort to invite technology entrepreneurs and their companies to commit resources (time, equity, product) and integrate philanthropy into their business.

We invite other companies to join us in integrating philanthropy into your business to improve communities throughout the world.

Over the last 15 years, the Salesforce.com Foundation has become a vital part of salesforce.com's culture — and has allowed us to engage our employees in their communities and support the effectiveness of the non-profit sector.

Since our founding, we have given over $53 million in grants, 580,000 hours of community service, and provided product donations for over 20,000 non-profits.

1% time

Successful volunteer programmes involve multiple components including team volunteering, individual volunteering, pro-bono service, board service, recognition programs, and outcome measurements. Consider all these aspects when developing your programmes to make it effective for employees, the company, and the community.

Encourage and promote employee volunteering by establishing a Volunteer Time Off (VTO) policy. At salesforce.com every employee earns six paid days off to volunteer and volunteering starts day one at our new hire orientation. A great place to start is to determine what causes your employees have a passion to support.

1% product

An easy way to start your philanthropic programmes is to provide your product or service for free or at a deep discount. How can your product or service contribute to solving a social problem or support a non-profit's mission? Check out the Salesforce.com Foundation's Power of Us product donation programme.

1% equity

It is important for companies to have guidelines in place to frame corporate grant making and employee volunteer programmes. This makes your programmes transparent to important audiences such as non-profit organisations desiring funding and employees who wish to volunteer. You want your grant programmes to support your local communities and non-profits, but they also provide an opportunity to empower your employees by giving them input into the direction of corporate and individual donations.

We currently make grants with a focus on: employee inspired giving including team volunteering activities and matching gifts; technology innovation through our annual Force-for-Change initiative; and supporting healthy communities in the locations where saleforce.com has corporate offices.

(Sources: Salesforce.com, 2014; Salesforce.com Foundation, 2014a; 2014b)

Discussion

On the face of it Boots' CSR approach looks the most 'strategic' in terms of Porter and Kramer's advice. It addresses areas where the company impacts on its environment (e.g. town centres and communities) and where 'competitive context' impacts on the company (e.g. marketplace as a 'key area' of activity). There is also evidence of a system of monitoring and reporting progress against a number of criteria, one of which is alignment to business strategy.

The Salesforce.com approach is more broadly based, aiming 'to help improve communities around the world'. Porter and Kramer might well object that an approach like this is likely to get 'stuck in the middle', and perform less well both for the company and its stakeholders than one which was more specifically focused on a particular cause or community. On the other hand, you could argue that this approach is more in tune with the kind of dynamic environment which contemporary strategists face. Salesforce.com dates from the turn of the century, in contrast with Boots' lengthy history. It may be that the highly flexible, unfocused, but employee-led approach is the right way to go for a company specialising in software and services – in spite of Porter and Kramer's advice.

So, yet again in strategy, there are no clear answers. But Porter and Kramer's challenge to evaluate CSR strategy on the joint criteria of its value to society and business has much power as a way of devising and justifying activity in this area.

Summary

This unit has looked in turn at some of the ways in which contemporary strategy scholars and practitioners are making sense of their subject. As we hope will be clear, while each of these perspectives on strategy has its particular emphases, they are not necessarily mutually exclusive. One could well imagine, for example, a linguistically-oriented researcher being interested in the way that small episodes of communication together contribute to emergent strategy in an organisation viewed as a complex adaptive system. Similarly, attention to elements of strategy practice such as language and stories may reveal how the workings of power in organisations mirror and reproduce the larger social structures of domination which preoccupy critical management scholars. A further point to note, as has been emphasised in our discussion of complexity, is that newer directions in strategy do not necessarily mean we have to abandon more orthodox perspectives. As we approach the end of the module, and you are able to draw together and synthesise the various points of view and frameworks you have encountered, you will no doubt find some elements of strategic thought more plausible and relevant than others, through the exercise of your critical faculties and bearing in mind your own experience and professional context.

Here is a brief summary of the main points we have covered in our treatment of complexity, discourse, critical management studies and CSR as perspectives on strategy.

Complexity thinking in strategy takes as its starting point the properties of complex adaptive systems such as flocks of birds, populations of bacteria, or organisations. The distinctive characteristic of such systems is that they can respond to their environments in more than one way. This makes them qualitatively different from mechanical systems (like central heating regulated by a thermostat), which are entirely predictable in their responses.

According to Pascale (Reading 18) complex adaptive systems are made up of many active members, operating at different levels. They thrive on a certain amount of instability, without which they tend to die. They can sense patterns, which help them to anticipate and respond to change. Therefore an organisation needs to avoid too much stability, and allow its members the flexibility to generate more complexity through self-organising activities. This moves them into a productive position 'towards the edge of chaos' where creative and relevant strategies can emerge. However, managers need to accept that there are limits to the amount of conventional control they can hope to exercise because of the unpredictability of cause and effect in such systems. Complex systems cannot be directed, merely disturbed.

Complexity's perspective on change emphasises interdependence as organisations and their environments continuously change together towards an unpredictable future – what is known as co-evolution. Such patterns of change are the result of interactions and relationships whose eventual effects may be out of proportion with their original cause. The timescale of such effects may also be far removed from their original cause.

Instead of the conventional emphasis on planning and control (usually through negative feedback) complexity approaches to strategy stress the role of managers as facilitators, creating the right conditions for effective strategy to emerge and building upon desirable developments. The capabilities which organisations need to develop to encourage the emergence of effective strategy are different from those associated with more traditional approaches. There is a greater emphasis on learning and sense-making, and less emphasis on control and objectivity.

One way in which members of an organisation interact as a complex adaptive system is through the many conversations that take place each day. This brings us to the second of our perspectives in this unit – strategy as discourse – which emphasises the role of language (in the broadest sense) to construct social reality. The way people speak and write in organisations rules in certain kinds of strategy and rules out others. We acknowledged the important role that story telling has in how people make sense of their organisational lives, and how this contributes to the development and implementation of strategy.

Strategy as a discourse integrates story and narrative. Stories have a plot – and usually revolve around a problem and its solution. Narrative is a broader concept – a way of knowing and understanding as well as communicating. It contains stories, but also signs and symbols. Stories and narratives contribute to the overall concept of discourse which, in organisational terms, means a way of referring to something which makes it acceptable. Discourse as a concept explains why some ways of talking about strategy are acceptable and others are not. To be taken seriously, managers and others need to adopt the dominant discourse.

Wrapped up in this notion is power. We described two types: 'power over' (a way of getting others to do what we want) and 'power to' (the positive kind of power that enables us to get things done). Knowing the 'rules of the game' in strategy discourse can be a source of considerable power, of both types. Also closely related to how discourse works is the concept of identity or self-image. Identity can help define the limits of a discourse as strategists are unlikely to act or talk in ways which contradict their images of themselves. Two further concepts which help develop our understanding of strategy as discourse are authority (conferred by position in a hierarchy) and legitimacy (earned by reputation or experience). Those in authority can use the power this entails to shape discourse, but those with legitimacy also need to be included in any discourse if it is to become acceptable.

The concept of power is also central to critical management studies – our third perspective in this unit. We underlined its position as a growing field of interest among contemporary strategy researchers (e.g. in the area of 'strategy as practice') and as a reflection of contemporary concerns about the effects of business on society.

We traced its roots to critical theory, as devised by the Frankfurt school in the mid-twentieth century, which sought to explain social structure in terms of domination by the powerful (reinforced through taken-for-granted aspects of culture). According to this view, management acts to reinforce and reproduce social divisions, as well as causing waste and environmental degradation. Against this view we offered the counter-argument that management is an innocent tool, but noted that there are contemporary concerns about its 'amoral' approach through an over-emphasis on technical aspects at the expense of wider effects.

Alvesson and Willmott, in Reading 19, outlined critical management studies' objections to strategy under three headings: strategy talk (the way that discourse about strategy acts to belittle views other than those of 'strategists'), the effect of concentration as the result of strategic efforts to defeat competition (stifling diversity and damaging the environment) and its 'political' effects (denying wider access to decision making in organisations, which might result in more societally beneficial action).

We criticised critical management studies on the grounds of its impracticality, noting the distinction between 'knowledge of' and 'knowledge for' management, but questioned how realistic this distinction is. We concluded that critical management studies, at least as articulated by Alvesson and Willmott in Reading 19, may be more complementary to orthodox but reflective approaches to management than is at first apparent.

Orthodox strategic thought as represented by Porter and Kramer (2006) responds to societal concerns about the impact of business by setting out principles for effective CSR. Convinced that business and society are essentially interdependent rather than in conflict, these authors urge the use of the same frameworks that guide commercial strategy to enable companies to identify and implement the most mutually advantageous CSR programmes, thus providing a counter argument to the pessimistic analysis of critical management theorists.

In conclusion, we must stress that complexity, discourse, critical management studies and attention to CSR are not the only directions in which contemporary strategy research and practice are moving. We also need to emphasise that they are by no means likely to threaten the dominance of the classical approach to strategy with which we have been comparing them (and, indeed, we have placed CSR as articulated by Porter and Kramer within the classical camp). For very good reasons most organisations continue to use frameworks and models which have their roots in conventional scientific thinking about the world, draw on economic rather than narrative analysis of behaviour, and take a partial view of the effect and responsibilities of business. However, as we have emphasised regularly through this module, such frameworks and models need to be put into practice with caution and a clear sense of their lack of universality. Some of the ideas we have covered in this unit will, we hope, help you to understand the potential gaps and shortcomings of more traditional approaches to strategy, and thus use and discuss them more critically and effectively.

Block 6: Conclusion

This block has dealt with some current issues in strategy – both in terms of how strategists establish a workable view of future circumstances, and through looking at some of the ways in which strategy is developing into the future as an academic endeavour and guide for practice.

In Unit 1, we examined quantitative and qualitative forecasting, noting the necessity of managerial judgement in both cases. We then undertook an extended discussion of scenario planning, taking into account the variety of approaches and applications of this technique – from computer-generated models of the future (with probabilities attached), to more humanistic attempts to transform management thinking through involvement in the development and use of scenarios (whose probability is irrelevant compared to their plausible depiction of diverse futures).

Unit 2 examined three areas of current interest among researchers in strategy, which we see as having potential to affect its future trajectory as an academic discipline.

Complexity theory has had an impact on a number of areas of knowledge, from the natural sciences (where it was originally developed) to economics and consumer behaviour. Its relevance to strategy is in the way it casts organisations as complex adaptive systems, co-evolving with their environments towards the future. As well as changing the way we think about the dynamics of environmental fit, complexity's perspective on organisations themselves as complex adaptive systems provides a rich seam of inspiration for managers concerned to avoid strategic stagnation.

Our second perspective, strategy as discourse, underlined the importance of language (uttered and written) in strategic practice. By regarding language as constitutive of reality, not just a transparent medium of expression, we can recognise how storytelling in strategy establishes patterns of power and identity, and lays claim to authority and legitimacy for strategists.

Our brief account of critical management studies indicated its debt to critical theory among other twentieth-century developments in social critique (such as feminism, environmentalism and postmodernism). Its criticisms of strategy include objections to the 'colonising' effect of strategic talk, concern about the effects of industry concentration as the result of strategic mergers, and a plea for more democracy in organisational strategy making. How practical such ideas can ever hope to be is questionable, but critical management studies reflects concerns about which managers need to be critically aware themselves. CSR offers a more orthodox, classical approach to harmonising the interests of business and society.

Module conclusion

Looking back over the six blocks of the module, we hope that you feel we have made some headway in our aim of making sense of strategy, though part of the challenge of doing so is that strategy, as a developing field, will always elude attempts to systematise it completely into one overall understanding. So if there are still some loose ends, that is only to be expected. However, we hope that you now have a clearer and more critical understanding of the breadth and scope of the subject, its powerful insights and its limitations.

We started out by problematising the concept of strategy in Block 1 *Introducing strategy*, depicting it as open to interpretation in a number of ways, and encouraging you to think critically about it from the outset. We also introduced a number of different 'theories of action' concerning strategy to which we have referred from time to time in subsequent blocks in order to help you frame your own critical understanding. Another important element of Block 1 was to establish the importance of strategy as something that people actually do; a social activity carried out at particular times and in particular places, rather than an abstract ideal process.

Block 2 *Strategic analysis* covered a number of influential frameworks and models that help strategists make sense of their worlds. We deepened our examination of the rival (but in many ways complementary) claims of the positioning school and the Resource-Based View (RBV) of strategy. We illustrated how either approach can be applied to a number of situations to provide an overview of external and internal factors relevant to the appropriate direction of an organisation. We emphasised the intricate nature of the internal and external environment, and the complexity of the network of stakeholder interests which organisations need to take into account. We also looked at some of the main issues presented by globalisation, the effects of which mean that no organisation can afford to ignore the potential of international competition.

Block 3 *Strategic choice* looked at the range of options broadly available to strategists. While our treatment of the stages of analysis and choice implies a sequence of activity, it is important to reiterate that this is a simplified picture in order to clarify the concepts themselves. Real life is a great deal messier. The frameworks we discussed from Ansoff (1987) and Porter (1985) help to clarify the kind of choices open to strategists at any point, but certainly do not indicate the right path in themselves. They can be useful, but are merely guides. Judgement, rather than formulaic approaches, is necessary in the interpretation and choice of strategic direction. As well as covering the levels at which such choices operate – corporate strategy to decide where to compete and competitive strategy to decide how to compete – we challenged you to think about what decision making involves, and how it might be done more effectively.

Block 4 *Collaborative analysis* invited you to try out some of these concepts as applied to a major case study, as a way of experiencing their strengths and limitations directly – if only in a simulated context. As we have tried to emphasise throughout the module, however, strategic thinking can have a direct relevance to your own personal and professional life, by offering you frameworks for analysis and decisions, which can be adapted to a wide range of situations.

Block 5 *Strategic implementation* helped consolidate your understanding of the problems that face those putting strategy to work, and how they may best be dealt with. We tried to cover a wide range of organisational factors in an attempt to expose how they can facilitate or hamper effective implementation. To some extent, this treatment of the subject, in order to communicate ideas with the required simplicity, necessitated us drawing a false distinction between implementation and strategy making itself. However, we hope that in the account we offered of the activity of different actors (senior and middle managers, and external consultants) we communicated the integration of strategy and implementation.

The final block *Contemporary directions in strategy* has looked at the way strategists attempt to envisage the future through forecasting and scenario planning, as well as offering some thoughts on where strategy is heading as a discipline. This involved using complexity, discourse analysis and critical management studies as examples of current academic concerns for researchers, which also link to how practitioners understand and carry out the work of strategy in the twenty-first century.

Congratulations on getting to the end of the module material. We hope this brief summary of the module has helped you take an overview of what you have been learning and will provide a basis for your revision in preparation for the final examination and, perhaps more importantly, your own productive exercise of strategic thinking in your personal and professional practice.

References

Adler, P. S., Forbes, L. C. and Willmott, H. (2007) 'Critical management studies', *The Academy of Management Annals*, vol. 1, no. 1, pp. 119–79.

Allen, P. (2001) 'A complex systems approach to learning in adaptive networks', *International Journal of Innovation Management*, vol. 5, no. 2, pp. 149–80.

Ansoff, H. I. (1987) *Corporate Strategy*, London, Penguin.

Barry, D. and Elmes, M. (1997) 'Strategy retold: toward a narrative view of strategic discourse', *Academy of Management Review*, vol. 22, pp. 429–52.

Bood, R. and Postma, T. (1997) 'Strategic learning with scenarios', *European Management Journal*, vol. 15, no. 6, pp. 633–47.

Boots UK (2013) 'Our approach', *Building healthy and more sustainable communities, Boots UK Corporate Social Responsibility Performance Update 2012/13*, [Online]. Available at http://www.boots-uk.com/media/App_Media/BUKCSR2013/Home/pdf/Boots_UK_CSR_Performance_Update.pdf (Accessed 28 February 2014).

Bradshaw, A. and Fuat Firat, A. (2007) 'Rethinking critical marketing' in Saren, M., Maclaran, P., Goulding, C., Elliott, R., Shankar, A., and Catterall, M. (2007) *Critical Marketing: Defining the Field*, Oxford, Butterworth Heinemann, pp. 30–43.

Burt, G., Wright, G., Bradfield, R., Cairns, G. and van der Heijden, K. (2006) 'The role of scenario planning in exploring the environment in view of the limitations of PEST and its derivatives', *International Studies of Management and Organisation*, vol. 36, no. 3, Fall, pp. 50–76.

Carlisle, Y. (2010) 'Change Management and Complexity Dynamics', *Henry Stewart Talks: Change Management series*, [Online]. Available at http://hstalks.com (Accessed 7 June 2010).

Clegg, S. R., Courpasson, D. and Phillips, N. (2006) *Power and Organizations*, London, Sage Publications.

Conger, J. (2006) 'The impact of strategic storytelling', London, Fifty Lessons Ltd [Online]. Available at http://openuniversity.fiftylessons.com.libezproxy.open.ac.uk/viewlesson.asp?l=433 (Accessed 31 January 2010).

Currie, G. and Brown, A. D. (2003) 'A narratological approach to understanding processes of organizing in a UK hospital', *Human Relations*, vol. 56, no. 5, pp. 563–86.

Day, G. S. and Schoemaker, P. J. H. (2006) *Peripheral Vision: Detecting the Weak Signals That Will Make or Break Your Company*, Cambridge MA, Harvard Business School Press.

Downs, A., Durant, R. and Carr, A. N. (2003) 'Emergent strategy development for organizations', *Emergence*, vol. 5, no. 2, pp. 5–28.

The Economist (2009) 'Managing in the fog', *The Economist*, vol. 390, no. 8620, pp. 67–8.

Fisher, W. R. (1984) 'Narration as a human communication paradigm: the case of public moral argument', *Communication Monographs*, vol. 51, no. 1, March, pp. 1–22.

Fisher, W. R. (1987) *Human Communication as Narration: Toward a Philosophy of Reason, Value, and Action*, Columbia, University of South Carolina Press.

Friedman, M. (1970) 'The social responsibility of business is to increase its profits', *New York Times Magazine*, 13 September, p. 33.

Greenspan, A. (2008) 'We will never have a perfect model of risk', *FT.com*, 18 March [Online]. Available at http://blogs.ft.com/economistsforum/2008/03/we-will-never-havea-perfect-model-of-risk/ (Accessed 31 May 2010).

In Our Time (2010) 'The Frankfurt School', BBC Radio 4, broadcast 15 January [Online]. Available at http://www.bbc.co.uk/programmes/b00pr54s (Accessed 31 January 2010).

Jain, S. C. and Tucker, L. R. (1995) 'The influence of culture on strategic constructs in the process of globalization: an empirical study of North American and Japanese MNCs', *International Business Review*, vol. 4, no. 1, pp. 19–37.

Janis, I. L. (1972) *Victims of Groupthink*, Boston, Houghton Mifflin.

Janis, I. L. (1982) *Groupthink: Psychological Studies of Policy Decisions and Fiascoes*, 2nd edn, Boston, Houghton Mifflin.

Jarzabkowski, P., Balogun, J. and Siedl, D. (2007) 'Strategizing: the challenges of a practice perspective', *Human Relations*, vol. 60, no. 1, pp. 5–29.

Kelly, A. (2003a) 'Income soars at Cancer Research', *Third Sector*, 5 February [Online]. Available at http://www.thirdsector.co.uk/Channels/Fundraising/Article/618675/Income-soars-Cancer-Research/ (Accessed 31 January 2010).

Kelly, A. (2003b) 'Newsmaker: head of a popular cause – Peter Cardy, chief executive, Macmillan Cancer Relief', *Third Sector*, 16 July [Online]. Available at http://www.thirdsector.co.uk/Channels/Fundraising/Article/615704/bNEWSMAKER-Headpopular-cause-Peter-Cardychief-executive-Macmillan-Cancer-Relief/ (Accessed 31 January 2010).

Krueger, R. A. and Casey, M. A. (2008) *Focus Groups: A Practical Guide for Applied Research* 4th edn, Thousand Oaks, CA, Sage Publishing.

Krugman, P. (2008) *The Return Of Depression Economics*, London, Penguin.

Landsberger, H. (1958) *Hawthorne Revisited*, Ithaca, New York, Cornell University Press.

Lempert, R. J., Groves, D. G., Popper, S. W. and Bankes, S. C. (2006) 'A general, analytic method for generating robust strategies and narrative scenarios', *Management Science*, vol. 52, no. 4, pp. 514–28.

Lorenz, E. (1963) 'Predictability: Does the Flap of a Butterfly's Wings in Brazil Set Off a Tornado in Texas?' Talk presented 29 December, AAAS Section on Environmental Sciences, New Approaches to Global Weather: GARP. Sheraton Park Plaza Hotel, Boston, Mass. [Online]. Available at http://eapsweb.mit.edu/research/Lorenz/Butterfly_1972.pdf (Accessed 29 April 2010).

Makridakis, S., Wheelwright, S. C and Hyndman, R. J. (1998) *Forecasting Methods and Applications*, 3rd edn, Hoboken, New Jersey, John Wiley and Sons Inc.

Mandelbrot, B. (1982) *The Fractal Geometry of Nature*, New York, W H Freeman & Co.

Marx, K. and Engels, F. (1974) *The German Ideology Part 1, With selections from parts 2 and 3, together with Marx's "Introductions to a critique of political economy"*, edited by Arthur, C. J., 2nd edn, London, Lawrence and Wishart.

McKelvey (2001) 'Energizing order-creating networks of distributed intelligence', *International Journal of Innovation Management*, vol. 5, pp. 181–212.

McMillan, E. (2008) *Complexity Management and The Dynamics of Change: Challenges for Practice*, London, Routledge.

McMillan, E. and Carlisle, Y. M. (2007) 'Strategy as order emerging from chaos: a public sector experience', *Long Range Planning*, vol. 40, no. 6, pp. 574–93.

Michels, D. (2009) 'Beware of optimistic forecasts', London, Fifty Lessons Ltd [Online]. Available at http://openuniversity.fiftylessons.com.libezproxy.open.ac.uk/viewlesson.asp?l=294 (Accessed 31 July 2009).

O'Neill, O. (2002) *A Question of Trust*, Cambridge, Cambridge University Press.

The Open University (2000) *B825 Unit 3: Planning under conditions of uncertainty*, Milton Keynes, The Open University.

Porter, M. E. (1985) *Competitive Advantage*, New York, Free Press.

Porter, M. E. (1990) *The Competitive Advantage of Nations*, London, Macmillan.

Porter, M. E. and Kramer, M. R. (2006) 'Strategy and society: the link between competitive advantage and corporate social responsibility', *Harvard Business Review*, vol. 84, no. 12, December, pp. 78–92.

Pascale, R. T., Milleman, M. and Gioj, L. (2001) *Surfing the Edge of Chaos: The Laws of Nature and the New Laws of Business*, New York, Crown Publishing/Random House.

Peacock, G. (2002) 'Opinion: a competitive streak doesn't suit this sector', *Third Sector,* 4 December [Online]. Available at http://www.thirdsector.co.uk/Channels/Fundraising/Article/613425/bOPINION-competitive-streak-doesn-apost-suit-sector/ (Accessed 31 January 2010).

Quinn, J. B. (1980) *Strategic Change: Logical Incrementalism*, Chicago, Irwin.

Ramirez, R. and van der Heijden, K. (2007) 'Scenarios to develop strategic options: a new interactive role for scenarios in sstrategy' in Sharpe, B. and van der Heijden, K. (eds) *Scenarios for Success: Turning Insights into Action*, Chichester, John Wiley and Sons Ltd, pp. 89–120.

Reynolds, C. (1987) 'Flocks, herds and schools: A distributed behavioral model', *SIGGRAPH '87: Proceedings of the 14th annual conference on computer graphics and interactive techniques*, Association for Computing Machinery, pp. 25–34.

Romanelli, E. and Tushman, M. L. (1994) 'Organisational transformation as a punctuated equilibrium: an empirical test', *Academy of Management Journal*, vol. 37, no. 5, pp. 1141–66.

Roxburgh, C. (2009) 'The use and abuse of scenarios'*, Strategy in Practice,* November [Online]. Available at https://www.mckinseyquarterly.com/ghost.aspx?ID=/The_use_and_abuse_of_scenarios_2463, (Accessed 13 November 2009).

Rumsfeld, D. (2002) *Defense Department News Transcript,* speech made February [Online]. Available at http://www.defense.gov/transcripts/transcript.aspx?transcriptid=2636 (Accessed 22 February 2010).

Salesforce.com (2014) *Integrated philanthropy* [Online]. Available at http://www.salesforce.com/company/foundation/ (Accessed 17 October 2014).

Salesforce.com Foundation (2014a) *Share the Model* [Online]. Available at http://www.salesforcefoundation.org/about-us/sharethemodel/ (Accessed 28 February 2014).

Salesforce.com Foundation (2014b) *Build Your Program* [Online]. Available at http://www.salesforcefoundation.org/about-us/sharethemodel/your-program/ (Accessed 28 February 2014).

Saren, M., Maclaran, P., Goulding, C., Elliott, R., Shankar, A. and Catterall, M. (2007) *Critical Marketing: Defining the Field*, Oxford, Butterworth Heinemann.

Schein, E. (2004) *Organisational Culture and Leadership*, 3rd edn, San Francisco, Jossey Bass John Wiley and Sons Inc.

Schoemaker, P. (2008) 'What to do with the scenarios', *Paulschoemaker.com* [Online]. Available at http://www.paulschoemaker.com/mediaclips/ PaS_Comp_ISDN.mov (Accessed 31 July 2009).

Schuster, R. (1906) 'On the periodicity of sunspots', *Philosophical Transactions*, Series A, 206, pp. 69–100, cited in Makridakis, S., Wheelwright, S. C and Hyndman, R. J. *Forecasting Methods and Applications*, 3rd edn, Hoboken, New Jersey, John Wiley and Sons Inc., p. 11.

Schwartz, P. (1991) *The Art of the Long View*, New York, Doubleday.

Skinner, P. (2005) 'Monitor your business environment and anticipate change', London, Fifty Lessons Ltd [Online]. Available at http://openuniversity. fiftylessons.com.libezproxy.open.ac.uk/viewlesson.asp?l=273 (Accessed 31 July 2009).

Stacey, R. D. (2007) *Strategic Management and Organisational Dynamics: The Challenge of Complexity*, 5th edn, Harlow, Pearson Education.

Templar, R. (2005) *The Rules of Business: The Unspoken Truth About Getting Ahead in Business*, London, FT Press.

Tickell, S. (2009) 'Creative thinking under siege', London, Fifty Lessons Ltd [Online]. Available at http://openuniversity.fiftylessons.com.libezproxy.open.ac. uk/viewlesson.asp?l=1226 (Accessed 31 July 2009).

Wack, P. (1985) 'Scenarios: uncharted waters ahead', *Harvard Business Review*, vol. 63, no. 5, September/October, pp. 73–88.

Waldrop, M. M. (1994) *Complexity*, New York, Penguin Books.

Whittington (2001) *What is Strategy and Does it Matter?* 2nd edn, London, Cengage Learning EMEA.

Whittington, R. (2006) 'Completing the practice turn in strategy research', *Organization Studies*, vol. 27, no. 5, pp. 613–34.

Wright, A. D. (2008) 'Consultants are strategists too you know: how consultants' knowledge co-constructs strategy', paper presented at Strategic Management Society conference, Cologne, Germany, October.

Yeoman, I. and McMahon-Beattie, U. (2005) 'Developing a scenario planning process using a blank piece of paper', *Tourism and Hospitality Research*, vol. 5, no 3, pp. 273–85.

Acknowledgements

Grateful acknowledgement is made to the following sources:

Text

Page 56: Downs, A., Durant, R. and Carr, A. N. (2003) 'Emergent strategy development for organizations', *Emergence*, vol. 5, no. 2. Taylor and Francis Ltd;

Tables

Table 2.1: Carlisle, Y. (2010) 'Change management and complexity dynamics', Henry Stewart Talks: Change Management series, http://hstalks. com. © Copyright Henry Stewart Talks. Adapted with kind permission of the author;

Figures

Figure 2.4: Porter, M. E. (1990) 'The competitive advantage of nations', *Harvard Business Review*, vol. 68, issue 2, Mar/Apr. Harvard Business Review;

Illustrations

Page 49: © iStockphoto.com/Brandon Laufenberg;

Every effort has been made to contact copyright holders. If any have been inadvertently overlooked the publishers will be pleased to make the necessary arrangements at the first opportunity.

Module team

The academic module team

Chris Bollom (module manager)
Roshan Boojihawon (module author)
Ysanne Carlisle (module author)
Christina Cataldo (module author)
Joan Hunt (regional manager)
Steven Little (module author)
Loykie Lomine (associate lecturer advisor)
†Geoff Mallory (module author)
Maureen Meadows (module team member)
Val O'Connor (module team assistant)
Terry O'Sullivan (module production chair and module author)
Tim Ray (module team chair and module author)
Howard Viney (module author)
Brian Webb (regional manager)
Nik Winchester (module author)
Alex Wright (module author)

Module production

Janine Aldridge (learning media developer)
Anne Brown (media assistant)
Debbie Crouch (graphic designer)
Vicky Eves (graphic artist)
Julie Fletcher (media project manager)
Lucy Hyde (proofreader)
Lee Johnson (media project manager)
Alex Keable-Crouch (media assistant)
Aniis Le Neve (media assistant)
Siggy Martin (licensing and acquisitions assistant)
Mahesh Patel (service delivery)
Deana Plummer (licensing and acquisitions assistant)
Helen Riddiough (learning media developer)
Ryan Rushton (proofreader)

Critical readers

Frank Campbell
David Newman
Tony Stapleton